ARRIVING WHERE WE STARTED

We shall not cease from exploration
And the end of all our exploring
Will be to arrive where we started
And know the place for the first time.

from 'Little Gidding' by T.S. Eliot

ARRIVING WHERE WE STARTED

25 years of Voluntary Service Overseas

Edited by Michael Edwards
With an introduction by Frank Judd

VSO *and* IT PUBLICATIONS 1983

© VSO and Intermediate Technology Publications, 1983

Published by VSO, 9 Belgrave Square, London SW1X 8PW, and
Intermediate Technology Publications Ltd, 9 King Street,
London WC2E 8HN, U.K.

ISBN 0 903031 93 0
ISBN 0 903031 92 2 (Pbk)

Typeset by Inforum Ltd, Portsmouth

Printed and bound in Great Britain by A. Wheaton & Co., Ltd., Exeter

Contents

Illustrations: between pages 104 and 105

Acknowledgements

The publishers would like to thank the following for the use of their photographs, numbering them in order of appearance: Jeremy Hartley for numbers 12, 18, 22, 23; Jenny Mathews for number 24; Fiona O'Mahoney for numbers 10, 11; John and Penny Horley for number 19. All other photographs were taken by VSO volunteers. The lines from 'Little Gidding' from *Four Quartets*, copyright by T.S. Eliot; renewed 1971 by Esme Valerie Eliot. Reprinted by permission of Harcourt Brace Jovanovich Inc. and Faber & Faber.

Preface

In 1983 VSO celebrates its twenty-fifth Anniversary. As part of these celebrations, and to show what volunteering means in practice, VSO and Intermediate Technology Publications have come together to publish this book. It contains the stories of 26 of the 20,000-plus VSO volunteers who have worked overseas since 1958. We wanted volunteers to speak for themselves; to tell their own stories in their own words. The brief we gave them was very wide: to write a personal account of their experiences as volunteers, and, where appropriate, of how these experiences had affected their subsequent attitudes and careers. The result is a book which reflects the widely varying backgrounds and experiences of the volunteers who have worked overseas through VSO. Past and current volunteers, young and not-so-young, farmers and university lecturers, journalists and technicians, doctors and teachers, all are represented here. In addition, the contributions reflect the way in which requests for volunteers have become increasingly specialized, demanding different skills and levels of experience. Hence, the 26 essays are arranged in chronological order of dates of service, from Martin Garner and Chris Tipple, two of the first eight volunteers, to many who are still serving overseas. No 26 essays can claim to be fully representative of over 20,000 volunteers' experiences. We have merely tried to give an idea of the very broad range of jobs that volunteers do, and the backgrounds from which they come. Overall, the impression is not just of volunteers learning how others live, but also caring about it. Not just caring, but wanting to see change occur; and not just wanting change, but being prepared to do something practical to bring it about. This is the message of this book:

through living and working overseas, to arrive at a better understanding of the way we live; to re-examine old ideas and question accepted attitudes; to explore, to 'arrive where we started, and know the place for the first time.'

Michael Edwards,
London,
July 1983.

Introduction
FRANK JUDD
Director, VSO

VSO is a story of people; of the hopes, disappointments, ideals, frustrations, imagined motivation, real motivation, successes and failures of 20,000 men and women. These are the volunteers who have served in almost every corner of Africa, Asia, Latin America, the Pacific, the Caribbean and the Middle East since 1958. It was in that year that a group of visionaries came together with the indefatigable and invariably challenging first Director, Alec Dickson, to start an organization, Voluntary Service Overseas. Critical to take-off was the backing of Inter Church Aid under its dynamic Director, Janet Lacey.

In our 25th Anniversary year we have invited some of those who volunteered to speak for themselves. But VSO is not just a story of the volunteers and their dedicated supporters throughout the United Kingdom; it is even more the story of those with whom the volunteers worked and lived and from whom they learned far more than they could give. Objective history will be based on the evidence of those to whom VSO responded. It is obviously the people who requested the volunteers and who usually provided their accommodation and allowances who can best say whether they achieved what was expected of them. What is striking is that despite the intensifying economic and political problems of the Third World, overall, the grass-root demand for volunteers shows no sign of diminishing. On the contrary, it continues to grow.

There is always a danger of institutionalization. Somebody identifies a need: an organization is established to answer it. Too quickly the organization becomes the be all and the end all; and the original need becomes therapy-tailored to meet

1

the needs and convenience of the organization itself. Dogma becomes a substitute for analysis and creative thought. The United Kingdom is littered with debris produced by this depressing tendency. To avoid this it is essential to keep measuring activity against purpose. Flexibility, adaptability and extroversion are vital, and techniques and methods must never be confused with objectives. The key role of the genuinely voluntary organization is its dynamism and drive; it should always be stretched, and it should certainly be cost-effective, not as an end in itself, but because of commitment to its objectives. That same commitment will demand administrative effectiveness in order to maximize performance.

What then of VSO? While there is never room for complacency it is nevertheless exciting that at the age of twenty-five its activities are still expanding. There are more volunteers in more countries, a wider range of professional and technical qualifications deployed, and an increase in local group activities, with a refreshing emphasis on public education both about the problems of the countries in which VSO is operating and about the inter-relationship of those problems with our own economic and social system here at home. Fund-raising is improving and VSO remains firmly among the pace-setters in terms of cost effectiveness. Significantly, it has recently become a membership organization, reflecting a healthy desire to be an integrated part of the community and not an impersonal, staff-administered agency.

Of more than nine hundred volunteers working in some forty countries at the end of March 1983, over four hundred were in education (secondary school teachers, vocational school teachers, teacher training college lecturers, tertiary institution lecturers, education resource centre workers and librarians); more than one hundred and fifty were in agriculture (agricultural extension workers, foresters, horticulturalists, soil scientists, seed improvement specialists, agricultural economists, agricultural engineers, teachers of agriculture, animal husbandry workers, vets, fisheries specialists); almost one hundred were in medicine and auxillary services (doctors, dentists, nurses, midwives, physiotherapists, occupational therapists, medical technologists, nutritionists); more than sixty were in business and social development (accountants, small business developers, co-operative workers, financial administrators, social workers); and one hundred and seventy-five were in technical services (auto mechanics, electricians, carpenters, bricklayers, engineers, hydrologists and other craftsmen or specialists). All these volunteers have professional or technical qualifications. In technical services alone the range is wide, from City and Guilds to MSc's or Doctorates with years of professional experience. The average age of the current volunteers is twenty-eight; the oldest is sixty-four and the youngest twenty. Well over fifty per cent of those currently serving overseas have considerable work experience in addition to their formal qualifications. All have attended orientation courses before departure. Those going to communities where the use of local language is important have received language training. Without including the considerable voluntary input to support many home activities and selection procedures, or the many contributions in kind, not least by airlines, the average cash cost to Britain of placing each volunteer overseas is £4,000 per annum. Host communities provide an approximately similar amount to cover accommodation and allowances; a guarantee of mutual involvement.

VSO sometimes is asked how its programme differs from that of a governmental or inter-governmental technical co-operation agency. After all, volunteers are not infrequently at least as well qualified as other expensive technical co-operation personnel working overseas at market rates. Different people within VSO will give different answers. Many would agree that the 'V' is about commitment to a living community, to the cause of economic and social justice and to international understanding. Few would argue that there is any intrinsic value in the hair shirt. Volunteers are asked to accept conditions of service comparable to those of local nationals doing similar work, because this places as few material inhibitions as possible between them and those with whom they are working and living. VSO has also come to see the 'V' as implying a long term resolve to work for more responsible attitudes in the United Kingdom towards the Third World.

VSO has come a long way since 1958. It is now well into its third stage. In the first it recruited school leavers for a testing experience in which their enthusiasm and freshness were intended to act as a catalyst for social development. These volunteers went abroad for nine months or a year, and most went to teach, sometimes in fairly élitist schools. This first programme was soon joined by a scheme for those who had just completed an apprenticeship. There is no doubt that some of these young volunteers did have a stimulating impact; many were themselves changed for life, both in social attitudes and their anticipated career patterns.

By the early 1960s, as increasing financial resources went into the programme, it became clear that with no indigenous shortage of the unskilled or unemployed, what those with whom VSO was co-operating in the field wanted most was knowledge and skills which could be shared. A scheme known as Graduate Voluntary Service Overseas (GVSO) was therefore started alongside what became called, in perhaps traditional colonial style, the 'cadet scheme'. Stage two was under way. Young graduates and others of the same age with different kinds of qualifications became a steadily more important part of the programme. VSO sent out its last school leavers during the early 1970s.

The end of the 1970s marked the beginning of stage three, with constantly more volunteers expected to have work experience, so that they could bring practical as well as theoretical knowledge to their posts. This chapter also marked the recognition that among the very best qualifications of all was the ability to train people in how things actually work and about the need for maintenance: hence the growing contribution by technical volunteers. All volunteers are now expected to serve for a minimum period of two years.

Yet whatever changes have taken place in the shape of the VSO programme, its twin objectives remain the same: first,

4

based on an unyielding concern for economic and social justice and for human rights, is to co-operate in building up the self-reliance, self-respect and self-generating human resources of the people in the countries to which volunteers are posted; the second is to build up here in the United Kingdom an understanding about the reality of the world of which we are all inescapably a part.

Success is not to be measured by what volunteers themselves do. It is possible for an apparently dramatic contribution to cause untold damage by making the local community more helpless and more dependent than it was before. Real success is the degree to which over a period of time – sometimes quite a number of years – local communities become more self-confident and less the passive victims of circumstance. A VSO agriculturalist put it strikingly: the real value of the agricultural volunteer is when he or she has a common interest with the people among whom he or she is living. His or her task is to win the confidence of the people, and slowly demonstrate that there are options, that choices can be made, that it is possible to do something about the situation and to shape the environment.

This requires exceptional people. It is at least as true as when Alec Dickson sent the first volunteer abroad that qualifications, however impressive, are not just useless without the right personal qualities, but potentially dangerous. VSO looks for people who are above all able to communicate. They must be sensitive, patient, resourceful, psychologically and physically robust, and with a good sense of humour. They must want to learn, and to make friends.

Economically, strategically, demographically and environmentally the world is locked together. Yet the contrasts between the industrialized countries and the non-industrialized remain as stark as ever. The so-called 'North', with only one quarter of the world's population – still enjoys eighty per cent of the world's income; an average life expectancy of more than seventy years; education for most people at least through secondary school; ninety per cent of the world's manufacturing industry, and some ninety per cent of the world's spending on research and development. Most of the people in 'the North' have enough to eat; 'the North' continues to dominate and manipulate, to its own advantage the international economic, monetary, financial and trade systems.

With three quarters of the world's population, the so-called 'South' has only 20 per cent of the world's income; its accumulated debt is 600,000 million US dollars; average life expectancy is fifty, with one in four children dying before the age of five in the poorest countries (17 million died in distressing circumstances in 1982); half the population has little or no formal education; more than one in five suffer constantly from hunger and malnutrition; for many, the food shortage is becoming increasingly acute. Some 800 million people are struggling merely to survive, without beginning to live lives of the sort we in the North take for granted. For them death is frequently a release from degradation, despair and humiliation.

All this is happening at a time of revolutionized communication. The poor are increasingly aware of their relative poverty, and the affluent can no longer claim ignorance of the poor. East-West problems may remain serious but no lasting security is possible in a world so top heavy on its North-South axis. In Britain we seek regeneration. To achieve this we must get our economic management, industrial relations, education, and technology right. But these alone will never guarantee our future. Ours is also a crisis of values. To turn our backs on the horrific injustice suffered by the South would be to undermine any hope of the renewed moral purpose without which the future remains bleak.

Sane and effective international policies on finance, trade and aid are desperately urgent. Yet these in themselves can do no more than establish frameworks. All systems and structures are inanimate. It is people who make things happen. We all know of archaic structures where exciting things are happening because there is imagination, compassion, drive and motivation. We also know of theoretically ideal structures

6

where nothing is happening because everybody is dead from the waist upwards. To be effective people must be motivated. To be motivated they must have the self-confidence which springs from the conviction that they have the knowledge and skills to do things for themselves. That is the relevance of VSO, whether it is co-operating in the emancipation of human potential in the Third World or helping to free the North from self-destructive selfishness.

1

MARTIN GARNER. Born 1939, Liverpool. Joined VSO in 1958 as one of the first eight volunteers to be sent overseas. Between 1958 and 1960 he worked at St Augustine's Secondary School, Betong, Sarawak (Malaysia), before undertaking a brief period of teaching in India. He then returned to Britain and was ordained into the Church of England, working in Northern Ireland and Toxteth (Liverpool), before moving to his present parish in Burton, Cumbria.

I HAVE in front of me a fading photograph of Charles Martin carrying mud in a wicker basket. Quite a normal occupation for a VSO you might think. For the Head Boy of an English Public School in a British Colony twenty-five years ago it was distinctly unusual. The task was levelling a volley-ball pitch behind the boarding houses at St Augustine's School, at Betong in Sarawak. Also fixed on my precious bit of celluloid are Chinese, Malay and Iban. Some of our pupils were older than ourselves. We worked as a chain-gang. The outstanding recollection of the picture is of mud, sweat and laughter.

Charles came from Lancing College near Steyning in Sussex, I from Hardye's School, Dorchester in Dorset. For me this opportunity came as an alternative to National Service. The P.T. master David Goddard, now Vicar of Shirley in Southampton, put the idea to me and I jumped at it. Apparently there had been some correspondence in *The Times* about 'The Year Between': the hiatus then being precipitated by the end of national conscription. Men leaving the forces with university places were obliging school leavers to wait a year before going to College. 'Could not this resource of youthful energy be put to good use,' wrote former Arctic explorer Launcelot Fleming, then Bishop of Portsmouth. Nigel Cornwall, Bishop of Borneo joined the debate. But the real accolade must go to

Alec Dickson whose brother Maurice just happened to be Director of Education in Sarawak. Alec was a whirlwind of energy, an attempter of the impossible, with the genius of inspiring others. He had worked on community projects at Man o'War Bay in West Africa, and in Europe had organized, out of nothing, immediate help for refugees escaping from Hungary. It was on that border of freedom that young people from Britain came to help; nobody sent them, they just appeared. They volunteered, and Alec Dickson was there to weld them into a team. That was where VSO was conceived, though it wasn't born until September 1958 and the robust baby had to wait another year for its name.

I first met Alec Dickson in the late spring of 1958. Because of clashes with school exams I missed the general interviewing and was called to see him at home. The contrast to the tidy Rectory I knew could hardly have been more startling. His home, in Mortlake, was knee deep in papers – correspondence, newspaper cuttings and books in the making were every-where. I didn't know how to cross the room to the snowed-in chair I was offered. The lighting was dim and the decor dark; I had the distinct feeling I was in the jungle already. But Alec Dickson was no fumbler in the dark; he knew exactly where he was going. He talked quickly, with fire in his eye, once leaping across the room reliving a party in Nigeria where he had sung: 'Daisy, Daisy give me your answer do', slapping his bottom as he rode his imaginary bicycle made for two. Undisputed Queen of this Thames-side bedlam was Mora, Alec's wife. She seemed oblivious to it all, the perfect county hostess, handing me a cup of tea and chunks of delicious home-made fruit cake: I was, after all, but a schoolboy. She was the authoress who has recorded those early days in *Sarawak Season*. Apparently four hundred had responded to Alec's letter to Public Schools; eight of us were very fortunate to be chosen – five for West Africa and three for Borneo.

During that summer we were briefed in London. We had a crash course in language learning, by the direct method, using Czechoslovakian for practice. Bishop Cornwall gave us good advice and warned us to take as little as possible; 'You can buy all your underwear out there.' Dr Fleming entertained us to breakfast at his Club. We were lectured at the Royal Commonwealth Society and interviewed for 'In Town Tonight' by the BBC. Alec Dickson's *coup de grâce* was the reception at the Colonial Office by the Secretary of State. He and I were the only two to drink orange juice! Even now I can see Alan Lennox-Boyd being driven away down Great Peter Street. He stood erect in his open-top Rolls Royce, waving magnificently until out of sight, for all the world as if he were heading an expedition up the Limpopo.

Back home in Weymouth I gathered the kit together, resisting persuasion to pack everything my parents had taken to the tropics. They were pioneer missionaries to Uganda after the First World War. They took forty-seven boxes; any one of which could be carried on the head. I was to travel by air! They used to dress for Dinner, and read Dickens. Discipline had to be maintained; an old colonial clergyman cautioned me not to drink spirits before six in the evening – 'We lose all our best men that way.'

September 18th came and the Borneo trio assembled at Heathrow. The volunteers for Africa were to leave a few days later. The first VSOs were Richard Matson, Charles Martin and myself. We flew to Singapore in those pre-jet days by B.O.A.C Britannia, 'the Whispering Giant'. The flight involved seven stops. At Beirut, a revolution was in progress and we were not allowed to leave the aircraft. In Baghdad, General Kassem had just seized power and we saw the unforgettable charge of Camel Cavalry across the Airport. Between Colombo and Kuala Lumpur an unexpected tail-wind brought us across the Malayan Coast just as breakfast was being served. 'Not much point', said an old hand, 'that's KL down there.' 'Goodness' said the Hostess, 'I must go and tell the pilot.'

The Dakota flight across the South China Sea was if anything even more informal – its door appeared to be secured by string. The Malayan Hostess served limitless platefuls of scrambled egg; I shall not forget her. I have two memories of Singapore.

My money belt was stolen and I was greatly embarrassed by a taxi driver. Being Sunday I asked to be taken from the Raffles Hotel to Church. The taxi man drove me to the Cathedral, which if my memory serves me right, has open arcades at the west end. Anyway, somehow or other, I found myself alighting from a taxi next to the font in the main aisle during the prayers on Battle of Britain Sunday, with everybody who was anybody on parade! The Raffles itself was sheer Imperial luxury: an experience to be collected, savoured only by the antique VSO.

We stayed a couple of days in Kuching at the Bishop's House, a vast rambling wooden bachelor aerie in spartan contrast to the Governor's 'Astana' on the other bank of the Sarawak River. Richard Matson left us for a community project among the Land Dayaks. I have never seen him since. Suddenly we were summoned to the Wharf, and Charles and I were off: down the river to the South China Sea, along the coast fifty miles and then some forty miles up the River Saribas. On the junk with us were chickens, pigs and half a dozen Chinese. We all ate from a common bowl in the engine room and we learnt to eat with chopsticks in record time. Hunger is an effective teacher, despite a long swell, engine fumes and sweaty bodies. I retreated with my piano accordian to the cross trees above the bridge where the roll was more accentuated, but the air was blessedly fresh. I dreamed of my great-grandfather sailing this coast in his tea clipper, praying for choppy seas to discourage the piratical Sea Dayaks. The coast is so flat it is very difficult to see where it is. As a coastal sailor myself I am full of admiration for those seamen who can pick out the mouth of a river in a mangrove swamp with no navigational aids at all. We had to cross the bar at full tide and then wait for the next tide to carry us up stream. As this was a 'regular' occurrence an enterprising Malay had opened a coffee shop in a hut on stilts at Pusa. As Charles and I sat in the murky darkness I had the surprise of my life. On the wall hung an out-of-date calendar advertizing, in Chinese, 'Players Please'. The grimy picture was indisputably of Weymouth Bay, and there was the Rectory I had left 9,000 miles behind. I believe God arranges the little things of life as well as the big, and I thanked Him.

'Betong' means swamp, which is a bit unkind since Betong Bazaar is the first bit of dry ground (relatively speaking) forty miles from the coast. Here the White Rajah had built Fort Lily in 1858. Here he took his stand against the Iban tribe and their great Chief Rentap; here the Malay came in service of the Raj, building their Kampong just downstream of their protector; and the people of the land itself were Iban or Sea Dayaks. Where people gather, there the Chinese traders come, and Betong Bazaar was a substantial community. Each of these groups had a primary school, using their own language and teaching English. The secondary school had to use English and this was where we came in. Our brief, at its simplest, was to help at St Augustine's School, to undertake any projects the District Officer might decree and, above all, to make friends.

You see, apart from the rare visit of the child of a government officer, the local population never saw a youthful European. The District Officer was treated with due deference, the resident hardly ever came to Betong, and who else was there? The Missionary was, I think, always a bachelor. This inevitably led to a blank in the experience of the locals and indeed to a dangerous assumption that if one were educated one would *ipso facto* live like a senior civil servant. We invited our D.O. to talk to our senior pupils one day. He described his position, responsibility and work. He then invited questions. 'What is a civil servant?' a pupil asked. After a little thought (he was an Australian army officer recruited after the Second World War) he said solemnly, 'You see, boys, I am your coolie.' They nearly died laughing. Bless him, he meant well, but his answer was utterly incredible. It was to bridge this gap that we set our hands.

This was where my photograph of Charles Martin was taken. We didn't just attempt to teach in the classrooms. We shared life with the pupils on the compound, in the jungle, along the rivers and back in their long-houses. Level ground

13

was needed, for building and for sport. So we levelled it. We 'chunkolled' away with our hoes like the rest of them. The thick clay had to be carried, so we carried it. We got filthy and tired and grew ringworm and all kinds of ulcers. The locals had never seen Europeans in this rôle. We bathed with them, planted paddy, tapped rubber, mulched the young trees, dried the pepper and fished the rivers. We shot and ate squirrels. We felled a straight tree and hacked out a canoe. We were guests at great feasts and heard stories in the dark of great spirits. Rentap was the local Robin Hood. We heard of his mountain fortress in Bukit Sadok. None of the lads had been there, so we made a great expedition to climb it, and later broadcast the tale over Radio Sarawak, whose news service had been inaugurated in April 1958.

It would be hard to evaluate what we did in modern Third World terms; then it was quite novel. One project which we know was of real use went like this. We were told to dig a hole about fifteen feet square and six feet deep. Over this excavation we were to construct a pig-sty. Any hole in Sarawak automatically fills with water. We were supplied with fish to breed, and were told to expect two pigs. Alas, only one arrived; nevertheless we were able to demonstrate to all and sundry a cycle of food. We gave all our scraps to the pig. The pig's refuse fell through the floor into the fishpond. The fish thrived and multiplied, and we ate them: a study in perpetual motion! That was until, at Christmas, in a rash moment, we decided to eat the pig. Its mate never did arrive.

On Ash Wednesday 1959 the Headmaster's house was burnt down; the kerosene fridge blew up, and in a wooden house on stilts that was that. We lost all but what we stood up in. To us it didn't matter, but to the Mission it was a serious blow. I have the highest regard for the Reverend Anthony Perry, now Rector of Presteigne, who took this catastrophic loss in his stride. I think at times I must have strained his patience to its limit; in some ways we were quite undisciplined – aged nineteen, and let loose in a fantasy world of Tarzan and Head Hunters. For weeks at a time (in school holidays) I would

14

borrow a canoe and disappear into the jungle. I'm sure he had no idea where I was and to be honest for some of the time I had no idea either. But with a river system like that one had only to drift down stream and sooner or later you would turn up at the estuary. I saw many enormous snakes, and crocodiles bigger than my dug-out. Fruit abounded and fish were for the taking. It was risky no doubt, but no more than a teenager in England with a 750cc motorbike.

I suppose VSO is right to have shifted its membership to more mature candidates with trained skills to offer. But there was something special about the comradeship I enjoyed with the young Iban of the Saribas River. Simply because I was their age, and because I had no real responsibilities, I was one of them. I frankly doubt if any other young Briton has so criss-crossed the Jungle Batang of the Second Division, from Saratok to the Ulu Ai. My special dare was travelling alone at night. The noises in the dark, the sensation of unknown company, the crashing of some animal following in the branches above one's head, the unexpected fall into a pool or the sheer poetry of paddling through the jungle in phosphorescent water, a bush shimmering with fire-flies, the black menace of a shadowy reptile launching down the mud bank at your side. I have to confess that I knew that my fair hair and white skin in the moonlight was enough to terrify the bravest Iban. I had only to drift out silently from under an overhanging tree to send a whole canoeful of men tearing back the way they had come. 'Gergasi,' they would shout 'Jagga! Antu!' They got their revenge when I was bitten by a snake, and they insisted on tying my foot to the rafters of the long-house.

A more proper sharing in the cultural heritage of the people came in the celebration of the Prophet Muhammad's birthday with the Malays, and in the Greetings of the Chinese New Year. It was the time of Hula Hoops and the Malays were particularly lithesome. The Chinese boys tried to teach us the fearsome Kun Tow. We pretended not to see the illegal cock-fights. The Iban took us away up river one time to share in the nubai, or fish regatta: gallons of stunning poison were poured into the water and the sport was to try to spear the fish as they were momentarily paralysed near the surface. VSO for me, meant a total sharing of life as I knew it, and as I lived it, as a teenager with an English *joie de vivre*. I developed an emotional attachment for the Iban which has never been replaced. I dare to think that there are Iban who cherish memories of an English boy who shared with gay abandon the luxury of their jungle heritage. My privilege was brought home to me by an Iban student, in Liverpool in 1979. He was from a long-house near Betong, but his father was in a high position and this lad, who was not born when I went to Borneo, has never known the jungle as I knew it. There is a tarmac road there now. He looked in amazement at my simple photographs. 'You know more of my people than I,' he said. *Heu tempora! Heu mores!*

Prince Philip visited Kuching in 1959. Ambin, Laus and Baling went with us, to represent St Augustine's School. The unifying power of the Commonwealth came home to me as, during part of an evening's National Entertainment, His Royal Highness sat on the Balcony flanked on the one side by a Bornean youth and on the other by an English boy. We like to think it was partly due to that conversation that the Prince became Patron of VSO.

I taught briefly in India and then came home to be ordained. I have worked four years in Northern Ireland and nearly a decade in Toxteth. For both these assignments my VSO experience was invaluable training. Willingness to sit loose to personal property, to appreciate people for what they are, to be acutely aware of one's shortcomings breeds a contentment of mind, an indifference to pomposity and patience with one's fellow beings who make the same old mistakes generation after generation.

In 1868 Charles Brooke became second Rajah of Sarawak. He wrote, in 1909, of the policy he had followed as he worked among the peoples of Borneo for sixty years: 'finding much profit by it, more in kindliness and sympathy than in a worldly point of view, by making them our friends, I may say associates, though they are of a different creed and a different colour; and how we gained their hearts by living among them and really knowing them, not as superiors, but as equals and friends.' He would have approved of VSO.

For my part I would but add, as I look back over forty years of intense enjoyment of life: to me there is no greater thrill than following Jesus. In the midst of the chances and changes of this fleeting world the Man of Calvary is unique. He gave His life for others. He volunteered to leave the safety of home for those in need. The Gospel tells the original VSO Story and in that faith and by that example I hope to live and die.

2

CHRISTOPHER TIPPLE. Born 1939, Heywood, Lanca-shire. He served as one of the first five volunteers in Ghana from 1958 to 1959, before returning to Oxford (1st Class Honours, Geography) and Leeds (1st Class Honours, Education). After a period teaching, he went into Educational Administration, working in Carlisle, Birmingham and Yorkshire before taking up his present post as Deputy Director of Education for Leeds County Council. In 1962 he was the first person to work on Alec Dickson's experimental 'home volunteer' scheme, which was later to become Community Service Volunteers.

WHEN the Sunday paper thudded onto the mat that spring day in 1958 I had no idea it was going to transform my life. I was nearing the end of three years in the sixth form at a small Yorkshire grammar school. A place to read history at Oxford, the first the school had seen in eight years, was in the bag; but it was not available for two years. Returning national servicemen had priority.

I glanced at the paper, but soon put it aside. There was

church to go to, cricket to play, a girl-friend to entertain. I would be nineteen in the summer. Then my father showed me a letter in the correspondence column. The Master of Marlborough College was exercised by exactly the problem that faced me. What to do with two vital years? He was urging that some scheme be devised to utilize the talent which circumstance had produced. I wrote that day and promptly forgot all about it. The letter which arrived weeks later from Alec Dickson, as much a stranger to me as the Master of Marlborough, was therefore a great and welcome surprise. Would I like to be interviewed for a completely new form of voluntary service overseas?

I don't remember the interview but it must have gone well because I was soon buying tropical kit and suffering yellow fever injections. I was to spend twelve months teaching in newly independent Ghana, along with two others. Three out of the eight first volunteers of 1958–9 were going to remote, up-river locations in Sarawak, so our teaching assignment sounded relatively mundane. It was not to be so.

Understandably, there was no induction programme; but there were lots of compensations in being the first. We were received by the then Colonial Secretary, Lennox-Boyd – he was a giant of a man with a great physical presence. On another occasion we were received by the Ghanian High Commissioner in London, who promptly took us out to a large and exclusive lunch.

The terms, £1 a week pocket money and all found, seemed perfectly satisfactory. I do not remember being particularly apprehensive about the prospect before me, although I had never even been on a day trip to Boulogne. As always my parents, who had themselves never left England's shores, gave strong support, no doubt concealing considerable worries.

The Ghana which awaited a distinctly air-sick Yorkshire schoolboy in the summer of 1958 was still in the first confident flush of independence. Nkrumah was everywhere. His statue stood on the sea-front in Accra with a slightly blasphemous inscription, 'Seek ye first the political kingdom and all things shall be added unto you'. His house (perhaps 'palace' would be a better description) was built in the hills north of the city during our stay in the country. Streets had been renamed, and his picture stared at you from every hoarding. Yet there was no antagonism to the British or a white face. On the contrary, there was universal friendliness mingled with some incredulity at these young white men who had simply come to help and not to rule or to trade.

The last Governor of the Gold Coast had been well served by the colonial civil service. Many administrators had identified themselves with the interests of the people and were sad, indeed reluctant, to leave. They had also governed a country in which peace had allowed commerce and education to flourish, and in which the framework of law and its practice had become well established. It was a fertile country for lawyers and a fallow field for the growth of schooling. These were the strands, had I but known it, which were to shape my life directly for the next few months and indirectly for very much longer.

One lawyer who had done particularly well for himself from the naturally litigious inhabitants was Mr. O. Private education in England had taken him well clear of the mass of his fellow Ghanaians, but he had a conscience and a desire for some measure of immortality. The fragile educational system of Ghana presented a perfect opportunity. Primary schooling was free and widely available, certainly in southern and central Ghana. Frequently staffed on the pupil/teacher system common in nineteenth century England, standards were often mediocre. Secondary education, however, was available only for those who could pay, though fees were subsidized either by the state or the private promoters of schools. There were far too few places to meet demand. Mr. O therefore decided to build and subsidize a secondary school in the township of Akropong. A civil servant who had identified himself very strongly with the country, was Mr. C, a former private secretary to the Governor. Africa had him in its grip, as it has had so many who go to live and work there, and rather than leave at independence he had taken on the challenge of becoming headmaster of this new school. He was to be our friend and support for the whole of our stay.

The school itself occupied a patch of land hacked out of the bush in the township of Akropong. Akropong stretched along the thin and ragged line of tarmac running north from Accra to Kumasi. The houses were generally of mud, baked hard by the sun and roofed with corrugated iron. There was no running water, the streets were lined by the ubiquitous open drains and there was no electric power other than that provided by temperamental private generators. Indeed, had it not been for the rust-pocked signs for 'Coca Cola' and 'Klim' (it was several months before I realized that Klim was milk, written backwards, perhaps because the liquid produced by the white powder was itself so hard to identify), one might have thought that western 'civilization' had yet to reach Akropong, although it was only forty twisting miles north of the capital. It was the sort of place in which £1 a week could go a long way.

Inevitably, because of the long distances to many pupils' homes, the school was a boarding establishment. Remarkably, it was for boys and girls, or perhaps I should say for men and women. Some of the students certainly appeared to be of English secondary school age. Others, who had no doubt had to work long hours to raise the fees, looked distinctly middle-aged. Birth certificates were unknown and no one seemed to press the question.

Although the school was new, the facilities in terms of equipment, books and specialist rooms were basic. The educational fare was, in retrospect, singularly inappropriate and traditional. I was very enthusiastic, however, and the students were avid for education, showing a universal keenness to learn which had disappeared from English education many years ago. The reason was not hard to find. Something which is free and readily available is rarely appreciated; something which is scarce and relatively expensive usually is. Moreover education, as the career of the school's founder proved, was the key to material success. Working with one's hands was not fashionable or profitable; working with one's brain could be. These attitudes were among the worst legacies of English colonial rule, and I fear they have vitiated Ghanaian society ever since. In so far as I and my two friends represented a model, destined for Oxbridge, extolling the merits of Shakespeare, Milton and the Cambridge School Certificate, we must only have reinforced these unfortunate attitudes. Ironically, the students were hugely appreciative of our efforts, and I for one never questioned the rightness of our endeavour.

At nineteen I was very adaptable and soon settled into what approached a routine in these strange surroundings. Days and nights which varied little in length through the months. The hot mornings which built up to spectacular thunder storms at noon. The myriad moths fluttering around the kerosene lamps at night. The night cry of a certain bird which can only be compared to the cry of someone being slowly strangled. Playing César Franck variations for piano and orchestra on the ancient gramophone as loudly as possible to compete with the sounds of the night. And a wealth of reading. For in Mr. C's library I had struck gold – all those books – Graham Greene, Ernest Hemingway, J.B. Priestley and Aldous Huxley which I should have read, but certainly would not have, without this year's interlude in my life.

And then came the first small signs of trouble, like the large cold drops preceding the noonday storm.

To me at any rate the founder had always seemed a distant and enigmatic figure. An extravagant chrome-decorated American car and uniformed chauffeur complemented the man himself, hiding behind dark glasses. Now his visits became more frequent, presaged by a cloud of dust as the car left the thin tarmac strip and bumped its way over the dusty laterite side road down to the stream and up to the headmaster's house, a long low structure with steps up to a veranda. Clearly there was a problem, but neither the one other European member of staff nor the African teachers would, or could, tell us what it was.

The news, therefore, came as a bombshell. Silence in the

21

classrooms was replaced by the hiss of repeated whispers. Each morning girls from the school carried the water in pots on their heads from the well by the stream up to the school buildings, and their jokes and chatter as they did so reached shrill new heights. Even the figures who disposed of the night soil, understandably swift and silent in their work, paused for talk. And it was not from Mr. C. himself that the news came, well trained as he was in the skill of diplomatic silence, but from the bush grape-vine which operated as inexorably as the 'tom-tom'. Disagreements between the head and the founder had forced Mr. C's resignation. Neither I nor the school ever discovered what these were, but they were clearly issues of principle. Just as the first few cold drops of the noonday storm quickly became continuous thunder on the corrugated iron roofs of the school, so the hiss of rumour and the chatter of gossip became urgent discussion in secret meetings, and calls to action.

And then it happened. The whole school went on strike. Not the teachers, which could have happened in England, but the pupils. Ignorance of the cause of the resignation was no restraint; the strike was a powerful gesture of support for a white man they loved and respected, even though his protagonist was black. The strike soon gave way to demonstrations and then a march through the town culminating in a rally on the open ground in front of the Head's house. To someone raised on the colonial images of *Sanders of the River* this was drama indeed. The staff joined Mr. C on the veranda as he spoke to the school with calmness and dignity. They must respect his decision. They must learn that to strike would mean that most would be taken away by parents or guardians and that precious commodity, education, denied to them.

The thundering noontime rains were usually orchestrated by vivid lightning. The next news when it came, was not the culmination of endless rumour, it was a thunderbolt. The founder had died. The circumstances of his death were as vague as had been the details of his earlier visits. He was not an old man. No doubt some older and more traditional students had invoked the fetish. Perhaps it was a heart attack brought on by the stress of circumstance, perhaps it was more sinister. This was a dimension of West African life I did not wish to probe, but it was there.

The school drifted back to normal routines. But the Head's decision remained unaltered, perhaps because he anticipated the approach which would be taken by the Trustees who succeeded the founder in ultimate control of the school. If so, he was indeed wise, as we were to discover to our cost. He left to develop adult education on the border of neighbouring Togoland. We continued, apprehensive about his replacement. His replacement was a puffy, sadistic Ghanaian whom we named Fido, who made life difficult for volunteers. I completed my twelve months in the relative calm of a girls' teacher training college staffed by German missionaries.

What effects did VSO have on me? It changed my mind about what I wanted to read at university and I have no doubt helped me to get a better degree and a better teaching qualification than I would otherwise have done. More important, it made me a better teacher and, latterly, administrator. The need to respond quickly to changing circumstances and crises – without the induction programme and field support network now established – helped me mature more quickly as an individual. It did not predispose me to teaching as a career; that came later, and only after other avenues had been explored. It did ensure that I would spend my life in a service type of job and not, for instance, following my father's steps as a businessman. As for the young people at school in Akropong, they got enthusiasm, commitment and the exposure to a young Englishman which must have amounted to an experience they would not otherwise have had. I think that if you asked them now about the value of their schooldays, a nineteen-year-old Yorkshire volunteer would probably feature somewhere on the credit side of a crowded balance sheet.

3

JOE OGDEN. Born 1944, Billinge, Wigan. Joined VSO from university in Manchester. From 1966 to 1967 he worked as a volunteer English Teacher at Kolenten Secondary School, Kambia, Sierra Leone. On his return, he took a PGCE and then worked in a variety of jobs, including spells with the Swedish Development Agency, with VSO in London and Bangladesh, and as a teacher in Vietnam. He is currently working as a radio producer with the BBC External Services.

THE THING about Yonibana was that their juju was much more powerful than ours, so rather than drive straight into the town we decided to hang around outside till the last possible moment to keep safe from it. What I couldn't understand, though, was why we were safe from it a mile or so away when it had already reached us in Kambia a hundred miles further back. It had floored our best player with a nasty attack of malaria and made the right-back sprain his ankle. Two key players already out, a slender 1–0 lead from the first leg, and here we were about to enter the lion's den and petrified right down to the studs of our football boots. Given the choice, my money would have been on Yonibana; especially after the next incident. Half the team had gone to sit on the verge while I, the driver, and the other half milled around the pick-up wondering how to kill time, when suddenly the centre-half screamed out and jumped up from the verge. The goalkeeper immediately followed suit and within seconds the whole lot were jigging about, shouting and grabbing at those parts that Mary White-house would prefer me not to mention. The rest of us looked on, astonished. Whose turn next? we thought. Mine?

Thankfully not. There's a species of ant in these parts that doesn't like being sat on, and its kamikaze troops had crawled up inside the trousers looking for a sensitive area to pinch.

And of course the first area they came across was particularly sensitive, which is why we were watching trousers descending faster than in any bordello or diarrhoea epidemic. The juju had got to us after all, so it was agreed we might as well drive into the town where at least there was some shade against the hot sun.

We were offered food but we declined nervously. Water was less easy to resist, and everyone's transparent friendliness gradually relaxed us so that by the time the match started we were, if not cool and collected, at least not rooted to the spot with fear.

My credentials for being the manager and coach of this school football team were somewhat fraudulent. I was a rugby player to begin with and hadn't a tenth of the athletic skill of my team. But England had won the World Cup that year and I was the only Englishman around, so I was made school football manager. If I'd known how important school football was – the equivalent of the second division in England – even my volunteer enthusiasm would have paled. That, though, is the beauty of being a young volunteer. Nothing daunts you, because you're so ignorant of the magnitude of the task that you launch yourself into it with such verve and energy that you win through and panic only afterwards when you realize just what it was you were taking on. And so it was in the classroom, in the maize field, and in the engineering workshop. On the whole we won through because we weren't tram-lined by previous experience and had the energy to find a way that worked.

We won through against Yonibana too. It was what the newspapers would call a 'typical cup-tie', more frenetic than creative and more wearing on the nerves than the muscle tissue. A 1–1 draw and we were through to the final, 2–1 on aggregate.

That was something else. If there was any juju involved here it was definitely on our side. Not that we needed it, because the five-thousand-strong crowd was on our side, the referee was on our side, and the linesmen would have been if they'd been able to push the crowd off the line so that they could run it. It's not that the referee wanted to be biased or had been nobbled by our lot. It was his misfortune to be refereeing the game on a neutral ground, which just happened to be in the town that was the mortal enemy of our opponents, so on the grounds that my enemy's enemy is my friend we ended up with five thousand strong and healthy friends. And two policemen. I should point out that there are two religions in Sierra Leone – politics and football. There are of course the more conventional kinds, but they don't generate anything like the same degree of passion; to borrow a well-worn witticism, football is not a matter of life and death – it's more serious than that. So if I were a referee with five thousand young, healthy people obliterating the touch-line and two policemen feigning myopia I think I'd side with the healthy ones too.

It was a bit of a shock though for the unwary volunteer brought up on a different version of sportsmanship, and the joy of triumph was tarnished with shame at the means. And more so because I thought we could have won the cup without help. Time and again I was confronted, as here, with a different way of viewing things that brought the reflex reaction of 'This is wrong because it's not how we'd do it' or 'This is right and better than we do it', when all along it was neither of these. It was just different.

It took us hours to get back to Kambia, where we paraded the cup triumphantly round the town, singing the school dirge and acknowledging the applause of the crowd; or, to be more accurate, some very slight applause, because it was way past everybody's bedtime and only the lunatic and the poet were going to jump from bed at that time; the third of that trio would have other things on his mind. A couple of laps round the town, then, and it was off to school to present the cup to the headmaster.

He appeared in his shorts and with his shotgun – he slept at the school to protect it against thieves and vandals and groups of hooligans who turned up late at night in a pick-up shouting and singing the school dirge. It took a while for him to realize who we were and to lower the shotgun, and when he saw the cup his Italian eyes lit up and he placed it, chalice-like, on the plinth in his office. I daren't tell you what it replaced or he might get excommunicated. If it's any justification, it was the first time we'd ever won it and we were a young school making our way in the world.

Most of the pupils were ordinary farmers' sons and daughters desperate for the piece of paper that would take them to a secure, well-paid job. Some of them made it; many didn't, including our star football player who was in form three for at least three years and never got beyond it. Some would say, therefore, that it was merely a factory for turning out failed misfits and rule-bound bureaucrats, and I've put those arguments myself over many a radical cup of coffee – but only about other schools. In my heart I can't feel that about Kambia. There was life and there was education there in spite of the obsession with certificates. The students developed their thinking skills, their language skills, and their social skills alongside a prodigious ability to memorize any exam fodder placed before them. Of course there are better ways and more relevant curricula, and many are now being tried, but at that time they wanted what I had to give and I wanted to give it.

In the end though they gave me more than I gave them, but in a funny sort of way I've continued to give it back. For instance, they taught me what cassava was – an elongated root tuber with a coarse red skin and a rough fibrous flesh. It's as common in the tropics as the potato is in the temperate zones; it is cultivated in exactly the same way, it serves precisely the same purpose, and it arrives on the dinner table in the same form: boiled, mashed, and fried. And the similarity doesn't end there. They both came originally from South America and they both became the poor man's staple in the countries they invaded, partly because they're an excellent energy-source and partly because they'll grow in the most inhospitable soils. If anything, though, cassava has the upper hand because you can leave it in the ground much longer, it keeps on growing until you're ready to eat it, its stems can be used like brushwood, and it will grow in land in which cereals would refuse even to germinate. Four years ago I watched it being planted in the denuded redlands of North Vietnam, where a pick was needed to break up the impoverished land. It had so little humus, water, or nutrients in it that to call it 'soil' would be dishonest; yet ten months later the cassava was being harvested and eaten for breakfast the following morning. It was a time of dire food shortage and without the resilient cassava many people would have been in big trouble. Nobody has ever researched it but it's a fair bet that cassava, and its relatives the yam, sweet potato, and taro, have contributed more to nutrition in the third world than any other source of food.

Kambia, then, first introduced me to cassava and to a multitude of other aspects of the tropics – culinary, cultural, and climatic. I've continued to try to give something back through my work on *Hello Tomorrow*, one of the most unusual programmes produced by the BBC, a development programme that eschews the international conferences, the economic strategies, and the political arguments. It accepts that these have a place but it believes that if they do have any effect it must be seen in the villages and the shanty towns and in what the people are doing for themselves. So when it finds a cassava harvester in the Caribbean it tells the Pacific about it; when it hears how Tonga is exploiting its tourists rather than being exploited by them it tells Kenya about it; when the prostitutes of Nairobi make a better life for themselves it tells Zimbabwe about it; and when a listener from Zimbabwe explains how to trap snails in a beer cup it tells snail-infested Western Samoa about it. And when it hears that coconut water is better at curing diarrhoea than a saline drip then it never stops telling everybody about it.

But above all, it doesn't think of the Third World as a problem. It knows that most of the people wake up in the morning and smile at their neighbour, wonder how they might make the most of their cassava crop, improve their latrine, fatten up their poultry, get rid of their rats, and keep their children healthy. And it realizes that a major preoccupation with many of them is who is going to win the football match next weekend. Very few adults wake up with the problems of the Third World weighing on their shoulders, most children will prefer to laugh with their friends than pose glumly for a starving-child poster, and the political meeting in the chief's compound is probably solving a family squabble rather than embarking on a radical analysis of power structures through the ages. The western images of the Third World are not untrue, but their simplistic focus shows only a small part of the picture, and when we interpret the whole by the part we impose our constructs on the subject and, given the chance, colonize it with our ideas.

The progamme, *Hello Tomorrow*, and its presenter, Paddy Feeny, get round this, as much as it's possible to get round it, by reporting anything that seems to work, whatever its political or economic complexion. It's clear from the letters that come in that the programme is reaching the people that development is supposed to be all about.

When I produce it, a healthy restraining factor is the people who help me. At my shoulder, although they don't know it, are Nguyen Van Thuc from Hanoi, Nurul Islam from Dacca, Charles Louis from St. Lucia and, most influential of all, Ibrahim Kamara and his many brothers who taught me so much as a volunteer in Kambia.

Ibrahim was wonderfully mischievous. My first job as Form Five's teacher was to put everybody's details in the register. In the process, Ibrahim showed me that everything was not as it appeared.

'Name?'	*'Bampia Bangura.'*
'Age?'	*'Seventeen.'*
'Name?'	*'Ahmed Bangura.'*
'Age?'	*'Sixteen.'*
'Any relation?'	*'We're brothers.'*
'Name?'	*'Ibrahim Kamara.'*
'Age?'	*'Seventeen.'*

I looked up, not having caught it the first time. 'Seventeen?' *'Sixteen?'* he offered.

'Sixteen? I asked, looking for reassurance.
'Fifteen?' he suggested.

We compromised on sixteen. Lesson number one was that nobody really knew exactly how old they were but, as with everything else, they were willing to haggle over it. At a guess the ages in that class ranged from fifteen to twenty-one, and rumour had it that the star football player in form three was twenty-six. I suspect that academic ability hadn't brought him to the school in the first place and it certainly wasn't what was keeping him there. He was the exception, though. You were generally allowed to repeat a year once only and if you failed the second time you were out, on the grounds that scarce resources shouldn't be wasted for five years if you can get away with wasting them for only two. But this didn't explain why there was a six-year age difference in Form Five and why several 'boys' in Form One towered over me and looked distinctly uncomfortable in their regulation blue shorts. Ibrahim again came to my rescue. He told me that age had nothing to do with when you started school. More to the point was when your father got round to thinking about it or when he could afford to release you; then he'd probably send a couple of brothers together, and if times got hard he'd take you away again for a couple of years. He also told me that Bampia Bangura and Ahmed Bangura weren't really brothers, at least not in the way I understood the term. They were from the same clan, and that meant they regarded each other as they would their siblings and supported each other accordingly.

It was the welfare state in practice if not in name, and the more I learned about it the more I came to respect it. Within the tribe and the clan there was a well-defined system of rights and duties whereby the well-off would help the less fortunate, the young would help the old, and the parents of one would consider themselves the parents of all. Seen from outside, tribalism is often regarded as a destructive force hampering political development and fuelling animosity, but it is the only effective social organization in the artificial nations created by colonialism. Set beside that, its disruptive effects in the second half of the twentieth century are minimal. Without it there would be chaos.

So too in the seemingly more sophisticated cultures of Asia. A technician I knew at a paper mill in the north of Vietnam resented having to work in this foreign land. 'I will return as soon as I can to my own country' – which happened to be fifty kilometres down the road. And a village lady who had suffered in Bangladesh's war of liberation against Pakistan had trouble grasping the concept of Bangladesh. 'Bangladesh? My desh (country) is Ratanpur (a village in the north-west).' It can sometimes be useful to generalize about the Third World, provided we always struggle to remember how various it is. What does exist universally is football, and the ability to interpret it like you've never seen football interpreted before. In Vietnam I found refereeing difficult because the style of play is best described as heroic (the resultant wounds were treated with tobacco). In Bangladesh I found supporting very difficult because my favourite team was WAPDA (have you ever tried shouting 'Come on the Water and Power Development Authority'?) and in Sierra Leone I found organizing very difficult because of my total ignorance.

I was not quite as ignorant, though, as my colleague who reckoned the inter-form competition was a good way to earn some money for the school. Great effort was put into constructing a banana-leaf fence around the town pitch and a collecting desk was put up at the entrance. About three of us paid. The rest of the town just walked through the banana leaves – not consciously cheating, just wondering what the hell this banana-leaf fence was doing round the town football field.

The final itself was between the popular underdogs of Form Two and the unpopular arrogants of Form Four, and by now, well-versed in the way the favourites were usually allowed to win, I planned my strategy accordingly. It took a lot of persuasion to get our gentle Indian teacher to agree to referee the match, but I was determined to see fair play and the only qualified referee around who could be trusted not to give a free kick every time a Form Four player breathed on a Form Two player was the extraordinarily honest Tommy. He agreed, and we got out the powdered milk to mark the lines. It was a gift from the people of the United States, who would have been surprised to see to what use it was being put; but when used as food it made many people sick and when used for marking football pitches it made many people happy. Aid works in mysterious ways.

By the time the final came round there was hardly a banana leaf left standing, so the crowd found their way in quite easily and they cheered the bare-footed Form Two heroes on to the field. Four of the arrogants had football boots and the crowd shouted at them so angrily that they were forced to take them off. This appealed to my sense of fair play. The first half went well because the heroes played out of their skins and got a goal in front, and the second half was going well until superior skill told and the arrogants equalized. The heroes, however, got back into the game and everyone's hopes were raised, including the two neutrals who desperately wanted to avoid a riot but weren't prepared to bend the rules to do so. Then fate, or rather the uneven pot-holed surface, took a hand, or, to be strictly accurate, an arm. The ball bounced violently off the hard ground and hit a Form Four defender on the arm. Tommy and I could see that it was accidental but a thousand or so other people were convinced it was the most premeditated vicious action in the whole of human history. Unfortunately also by this stage in the game most of the powdered milk had been scuffed away, so while two of us thought the incident had occurred outside the penalty area, the majority were of a different mind.

Tommy waved play on, the crowd were enraged, and the headmaster, who was sitting with two dignitaries on the touchline, walked on to the field and stopped the match. He picked up the ball, put it on the penalty spot, and beckoned a Form Two player to come and kick it. I remonstrated with him and he countered, 'There is always an external authority that a decision can be referred to.' 'Not on the football field. The referee is always right.' 'In England, yes,' he said, and ordered Tommy to take up his position. The crowd charged on, surrounded the penalty area and the back of the goal, and the goalkeeper wondered why he hadn't been a centre-forward like his brother said he should. Tommy whistled, the hero ran up, gave the ball an almighty kick and it floored a spectator three yards outside the goal. Divine justice, I thought. Not so. The headmaster ruled the kick out of order because the hero was put off by the crowd. The second attempt was more successful and everybody went home happy except a gentle Indian who vowed never to referee another football match in his life and a raw volunteer who vowed never to organize one. Neither of them, as it turned out, lived up to their vows.

It wasn't only on the football pitch that different systems of values rubbed up against one another. It happened also in the classroom, in the mammy-wagon, in the market, in the church, and in the bar. Sometimes it showed up the faults in my native culture, sometimes the faults in my hosts' culture; sometimes it affirmed the strengths of mine, sometimes the strengths of theirs; and in the end it added up to an affirmation of both and an agreement to differ. With mutual respect.

This experience killed once and for all the picture of Africa as *tabula rasa* waiting for the white man's imprint and the picture of the African as an eager recipient of the white man's wisdom. In many ways he's got it more right than we have and his wisdom, developed over the centuries and imparted with his mother's milk, does not yield easily. As my neighbour the cloth-seller once said, 'Europeans are too weak to do anything but penwork, and they're so poor they can only afford one wife.' How do you argue with that, and still less with his unshakeable belief in the innate superiority of the African and his explanation of why that superiority hasn't made him boss of the world?

'How de dunya? (How's the world?)' he greets you. You reply, 'Fine-o, how de dunya?' And invariably he smiles and retorts, 'Black man no 'gree.' An unmistakable implication that were black men to cease their petty squabbling and start agreeing with one another then they'd rule the world. That's one man I'm not going to try and convince that I have a better way.

4

IVY HILL. Born 1904, Golborne, Lancashire. Ivy spent forty years in the library service, becoming chief librarian of Castleford, before volunteering through VSO in 1966. She served with the Zambian library service in Lusaka between 1966 and 1968, before re-volunteering for another three years with the Ghana Library Board in Accra. Since returning to the UK in 1973, she has been organizing private school libraries, lecturing and travelling. Ivy writes that 'I hope I am growing old gracefully in what is still a beautiful world.' She was awarded the M.B.E. in 1978 for services to VSO.

I RETIRED after forty years in Local Government, as a Librarian and Curator, and eventually felt I must give something back, voluntarily, to the profession which had given me so many happy years. I had heard of VSO and so applied to join. At the London interview I discovered I was the first 'senior citizen' to be enrolled for work overseas. It was fascinating being interviewed, instead of conducting an interview, and I quite enjoyed the experience. Very soon I found myself en route for Zambia, and the great adventure began. My first joy was an enforced stay in Nairobi, Kenya, where I contacted the City Librarian, a colleague from my Lancashire days, and was able to have a quick look around this lovely spot.

My first impression of Lusaka, from the air, was of a city in a blue gown, for it was set amidst jacaranda trees. I had a wonderful reception from the staff and members of the Zambia Library Service and this delightful friendliness was ever present throughout the whole of the time I spent in Zambia.

My first project was as a Training Officer, attached to the Zambian Library Service, and I arranged, conducted and lectured at various courses of study for Zambian librarians. The first course was for librarians from the various libraries in Lusaka – public, university, college, and private. The second course was residential, for librarians from all over the country (outside Lusaka), expenses being paid by the Ministry. Other courses were for members of the Zambian Library Services, which had branches all over the country.

It was a joy to do this work, meeting young librarians who were all so very keen for information, anxious to gain new knowledge, and pass their examinations. I do believe they would have stayed all night at the College asking questions on classification, cataloguing, routine, organization, reference work and so on, had I stayed to help. My regard for them was high. They were cheerful and courteous, yet had to struggle so hard for so little.

The second part of my VSO project was closer to my heart, for it was pioneering work. I was appointed Regional Librarian for the Eastern Province, an area about the size of England, with headquarters at Chipata. I shall always call it 'my Province,' for I covered thousands of miles of bush roads by Land Rover, establishing small Library Centres in remote areas of the countryside. I shall always remember the four-hundred mile journey from Lusaka to Chipata, only the first fifty miles of which were paved. I had two Zambian drivers, a 'Book-Mobile' filled with books, and my car, loaned to me by the British Council primarily for use in Lusaka. As Training Officer, I had much travelling to do. I was also organizing the Periodicals Library at the Unesco offices and training a local assistant for them.

We stopped the first night at Katchalolo Rest House, an historic spot, as I later discovered when reading up the history of old 'Northern Rhodesia'. For the first time, I heard the haunting music of the African bush, with its animals and insects, and caught the night fragrance of its trees and flowers.

A great yellow moon was climbing slowly up to heaven, and the earth took on an ethereal glow. Yes – the spellbinder had bewitched me!

After arriving in Chipata, my first job was to open a small library in Kapata, the African township, and train some local staff. My second job was to supervise the erection of the Regional Library in Chipata to serve as headquarters for the Province. While this was under construction I started to establish Library Centres all over the Province. Whenever a request came in for a Library Centre, I would visit the site and assess whether the request was justified in terms of population and local conditions.

What a diversity of places, each one so very different. Secondary, middle and primary schools, hospitals, missions, prisons, 'bomas', immigration points, agricultural camps, research centres, literacy centres, even a beer hall in a remote spot in the middle of an African village. I loved to sit with the readers in the delightful room made available by the beer hall proprietor, talking and listening while time slid by. It is surprising how frustration flies away when time flies with it. I was nicknamed 'Madam', 'Mrs', or 'Dona Buku' – 'Mrs Book'!

Many pictures still live in my mind, especially the great joy on people's faces when books arrived. They had usually written down questions to ask me, and the longer I would stay, the happier they would be. Although they so often had little to give, I always left with some gift of oranges, limes, grapefruit, mangoes, paw-paws, bananas, plantains or other items from their own smallholdings. Sailing over the Luangwa River in a thin blade of a boat, past a school of hippos, with my books, my driver, and the old boat man, all the inhabitants of the village would wait for me on the other side and form an escort to the centre of the village. There was the never-ending delight of glorious coloured orchids in the bush. There were prison libraries; one in particular where I was always asked to speak to the prisoners, and where they were allowed to ask questions and request special books for study. I can still hear the great prison gates clanging shut as I went in and out. My best centre-librarian in the Province was a prisoner and the greatest absconder the Province ever had! How I wished for more like him – never a missing book.

Then there were the schools, where I often spoke to ten classes during my visit on the subject of the books I had taken with me, and then waited for their questions; the secondary school where I always needed notice of what literature the students wished me to speak on, so that I could do my home-work beforehand, for the students were brilliant and literature was alive for them. Looking for cave drawings after a busy day at school and then a delicious meal with the headmaster and his little family. Sleeping at a far-flung mission house in the heart of the bush with only a wire netting door between me and the wildlife in the bush. Waiting on valley roads for elephants to cross before we could proceed. Wild dogs chasing the Land Rover for miles. Running over snakes and guinea fowl. The happiness at the agricultural camps, where I found many workers studying. I always left with a chicken or with eggs; indeed, my driver had a small poultry farm by the time I left for home!

More memories. A journey through lion country to a far-flung school which seldom had any visitors, and the pleasure and appreciation of the pupils that I had made the journey, and taken them books and spent a little while with them. Then the lovely cold drink from their store and the return journey with a swat in one hand and a tin of fly repellant in the other to chase away the tsetse fly. And then the peace of reaching the comfort and welcome at the Government Rest House at Lundazi Castle; and my own much loved 'chama'[1] too. And the Library Centre there, and how well I was cared for by the Zambians and Indians – over two hundred miles from my headquarters in Chipata, yet I felt safer than I would in any of our cities. During one holiday period I made a fact-finding visit by Land Rover to Barotseland to look at library-centres: four hundred miles from Chipata to Lusaka, then five hundred miles from Lusaka to Mongu, which I made my base.

[1] A 'chama' is a house-cum-smallholding.

My final appointment, and one which I treasured, was being called to State House, Lusaka, to meet His Excellency Dr Kaunda, who was greatly interested in my work. I left with the happiness of passing over to a newly qualified Zambian Librarian the work I had started in the Province, based at a delightful new Regional Library set in a lovely garden. I knew that sound foundations had been laid. Happy Zambian Days.

Later I made two tours of Ghana in West Africa, utterly different from Zambia, yet quite as interesting and delightful. I found its people kind and cheerful, and though, again, they often possessed little they always shared what they had. And again, I found the utmost courtesy and friendliness.

My first project was in Ashanti, as a College and School Library Officer with my headquarters in Kumasi. It was delightful work to organize and reorganize libraries at all the colleges and schools, working with the staff and students and training library clerks. There is a thrill in being given an empty room and making a library from it. The sorting, classifying and cataloguing of the books in progress, while at the same time the local carpenter is making the furniture according to instructions – shelves, cupboards, tables, chairs, issue desk and trays. Then the forming of the catalogue and the labelling of the stacks and shelves, followed by the putting up of pictures, pieces of African sculpture and flowers – beautifying the place with the whole college or school taking great interest and joy in every step. Finally, the explanation of the library and catalogue to the staff and each form in turn. It was worth all the long hours of work to see the joy on a student's face when s/he could go to the catalogue and find in it the author and title or subject of the book s/he wanted, and then by following the simplified Dewey Classification, go to the shelves and find the exact book amidst so many.

I classified so many books in the Ashanti Region that I *thought* Dewey Classification! At the end of the day I would sit with a sun-downer and look at the garden, trees, flowers and birds, but all would be 635, 582 and 598! I chuckle when I think of my garden boy's face on one occasion at my house in St Louis, Kumasi. He wanted to know what work to do next in the garden and I said without thinking, '634, please Samuel'; or, in English, 'Outdoor tomato plants please, Samuel!'

I was able to write a guide to the organization of college and school libraries for the use of tutor librarians and library clerks, and also conducted courses of lectures for them in Kumasi. My second job was to take my Ashanti scheme to the other regions of Ghana. The Upper Region from Bolgatanga, Northern Region from Tamale, Brong Ahafo Region from Sunyani, Volta Region from Ho, Eastern Region from Koforidua, Western Region from Sekondi, Central Region from Cape Coast, and of course, the Greater Accra Region from Accra. I visited every college, school and technical college, explaining the scheme, getting things going, and helping to train and select library clerks. This involved a great deal of travelling, but the results were always rewarding: the knowledge that sure foundations had been laid, and that head teachers, staff, and students were satisfied.

I always agreed to present the prizes or make a speech at speech days, and often gave the sermon at Sunday Schools. Each Region was different, with its own tribe, creed or race, yet I always found gentle courtesy and happiness in my work with them. During college and school holidays I lectured at the Department of Library Studies, University of Ghana, Legon. I also made time, as a retired Curator, to visit all the fascinating coast castles from Half Assini to Keta!

I came home from Zambia and Ghana like Marco Polo, laden, not with bags of gold, but with a host of happy memories of friends in all walks of life. All you who retire in good health and have the necessary qualifications for your work, put on your thinking caps and hie you to Belgrave Square, London, to see if you can help these grand people, calling for help and understanding all around the world.

I am ever grateful to VSO for allowing me the privilege of serving in Zambia and Ghana. My sorrow was that at seventy, I found it was easier to insure a supertanker for service at sea than send a woman to work overseas. That put an end to my hoped-for posting to Malaysia. Indeed, I still do not see why the age limit for VSO should be seventy if one is in good mental and physical health, for surely there is wisdom as well as knowledge, and wisdom is bought in the market of life.[1] Every volunteer comes to know the real meaning of the word 'service' – for others. A great truth I was taught in my work was that the thing we fear most is really fear itself. All one needs to do is to put one's life in the Hand of God, and trust, and all is well, and fear retreats.

5

GEORGE HORN. Born 1937, Plymouth. Worked for British Rail before training as a nurse (RMN, 1968). From 1968 to 1970 he worked as a volunteer on the Leprosy Control Project in Addis Abbaba, Ethiopia. On his return, he was employed as a staff nurse at Moorhaven Hospital, South Devon, and then went to Malawi to work for LEPRA. He now lives and works in Plymouth, where he is secretary of the local VSO Group.

THE AIRCRAFT began to lose height as the Captain told us that we would be landing in about twenty minutes' time. We began to turn to port before straightening out for the final rush along the runway. The engines were put into reverse thrust and slowly we came to a halt, and taxied to the arrival apron. Reaching the aircraft door I stood looking out over the Entoto Hills which surround Addis Ababa, the capital of Ethiopia, and felt the heat of Africa for the first time.

Despite the long flight I was wide awake and full of the

[1] *Editor's note:* VSO's age limit has now been set at 65, simply because of the difficulties in obtaining adequate insurance for those of retirement age.

sensations of my new surroundings, as Mike Barrett of the British Council[1] drove me through the city to the Leprosorium, about fifteen miles outside Addis Ababa. At the Leprosorium I met Dr Ernest Price, the Director of the Leprosy Control programme, and after the formal introductions, Mike Wood (another VSO who worked in the programme's laboratory) took me to my new home in the grounds of the hospital. We then went on a brief tour of the Leprosorium, and it was here that I met my first leprosy patient. We were walking along one of the many paths, when a man approached and greeted us in the traditional manner with a bow, holding out his hand for me to shake. I looked at the face and saw the swollen lips and distorted nose, and then his hands; there was only a stump. Momentarily I shrank with horror. Then, looking into his smiling face, I grasped hold of his wrist: my initial fear of leprosy had been overcome. I was told that the moment of fear was natural among people who were not accustomed to close contact with leprosy.

A week later I set out with Ben Hopper, the Senior Leprosy Control Officer, on a tour of Provincial Leprosy Clinics that was to take us three weeks, along two thousand kilometres of roads. The aim of the tour was to pay the field staff their salaries and to check their records. We set off on a Saturday afternoon and travelled north to Gojjam and Tigre province. During the journey north Ben had explained my future role. I had been going to be in charge of a group of clinics attached to the Ethiopian Coptic Church. These were run by two deacons who had been trained in the treatment of leprosy in Addis Ababa. Unfortunately a civil war broke out in the area before the programme could be started, and my Ethiopian Deputy Control Officer felt it too dangerous to assign me to the Coptic Church project. Instead, I was to take control of twelve leprosy clinics, with around 1,500 registered patients.

[1] VSO programmes used to be supervised in the field by the British Council. In all but a handful of countries this is no longer the case, and volunteers are supervised by resident VSO field staff.

We arrived in Dabat on the Monday afternoon and arranged to stay at the local Health Centre, where we saw some of the work that was being done. The following day, Ben said, we should ride together to the Semian Mountains.

'Morning m'boy, time to go.'
'Ah, um morning Ben, Mengesha, Gedafaw.'[2]
I lay on the bed trying to get my bearings, then washed and dressed quickly, and joined Ben and the others outside, making preparations for the day. Our point of departure was to be a small town called Debarak, where four horses – for Ben, Ato Legess (the supervisor), myself, and the local health worker – were waiting for us. Before this trip the nearest I had been to a horse was on Dartmoor, near to my Devon home. I looked at my horse with apprehension – it was huge. The local Ethiopians had been told by Ben that this was to be my first ride on horseback, and so the word soon spread, and a small crowd gathered to see the fun. Ben showed me how to mount the horse, by placing one foot in the stirrup, facing the horse's head. I was then supposed to hoist myself onto the animal's back. While I was given a leg up, nobody had told me I was to sit on the saddle, and so I very nearly fell over the other side. It was turning into a scene from a comical Western film; more through panic than skill I grabbed the horse's reins, promptly pulling its head back and making it rear. Luckily for the horse, help was at hand, and I was shown the correct way to hold and manoeuvre the reins.

We soon set off into what is the highest mountain range in Ethiopia. The higher we climbed the more impressive the views became, and the farther into the mountains we travelled the greater became my confidence in my horsemanship. After about two hours' riding we reached a small hamlet, where we were greeted by the leprosy patients. We dismounted and returned their greeting while the control staff got on with the

[2] Mengesha and Gedafaw were two health workers accompanying Ben and George on their trip.

task of treating them. While the clinic was in progress, Ben started to teach me about leprosy – why, for example, it was essential to examine the patient's entire body since the symptoms of the disease could show up anywhere. Foot ulcers were particularly common, but unfortunately could not be properly treated because of the lack of funds. All that the control staff could do was to advise the patients to keep the wounds clean. The main treatment for leprosy at this time was Dapsone, supplied free to the patients by UNICEF. A register was kept of the patients, and any new cases entered. The clinic finished, we rode further into the mountains and visited another small village. It was decided that, as this was my first ride, the two health workers and I would return to Debarak, while Ben and the others went on to visit the other clinics in the area. We watched them ride over the ridge and then we made our leisurely way back. Occasionally I walked while one or the other health workers would ride. I was beginning the process of learning how to walk very long distances.

During those three weeks of training, I learnt a lot about the work of leprosy control in Ethiopia (and also about myself). I learned how important it was to take water with us even when visiting clinics that were near to the centre. I was not supplied with transport (a Land Rover) since it was not Leprosy Control's policy. I was glad of this because I learned much more about the Ethiopian people and their way of life. In those first three weeks I lost three stone in weight, a result largely of the switch from three to two meals a day.

My first tour ended two days before Christmas 1968. Two weeks later, I set off for my second tour, this time under the guidance of Ato Bajaw, the Deputy Leprosy Control Officer. He had been briefed by Dr Price to speak to me only in Amharic after we had left the capital, as a preparation for my role with the Ethiopian Churches. Unfortunately we were not to complete the trip, because of the outbreak of civil war in Gojjam, after the imposition of heavy taxes by the Government of Emperor Haile Selassie. The trip was one long lesson in Amharic. At first it was hard work, and quite often I did not know what on earth anyone was talking about. But, one night around the camp fire, Ato Bajaw and the others were talking about the civil war. Much to my surprise, I found I could understand a little of what they were saying. At first I said nothing, then I quietly asked Bajaw where the fighting was taking place. The men sitting around the fire stopped talking and looked at me. Bajaw said, 'I thought you could not speak our language.' I told him that I could not speak Amharic, but was now managing to pick up some words and had made a guess which proved to be right.

The following day we arrived at another village where we were stopped by the police from going any further. Fighting was taking place nearby, and the police were either not happy with my presence, or could not guarantee my safety. So, sadly, we had to return to Denjen, the nearest place with a telephone. We contacted Dr Price who met us a few days later and drove with us to Debre Marcos, the capital of Gojjam province. Dr Price then had a discussion with Ato Bajaw and my fate was sealed. I was to be based in Debre Marcos, and my work with the churches was being postponed until the fighting had stopped. Unfortunately, the fighting never did stop during my time in Ethiopia. It was in fact one of many small incidents that were to lead to the eventual overthrow of the Emperor in 1974.

My home in Debre Marcos was very sparse, constructed with a wooden framework covered by mud and wattle. The house was divided into three rooms, a large room which became my main living room, with a cow-dung floor resurfaced with local material every month by my house girl. The only problem was fleas, which I soon solved with the help of DDT powder. I kept one room as my bedroom, furnished with an iron bed and a wardrobe borrowed from a missionary who lived next door. I also had a three-ring calor-gas stove, on which, aided by a pressure cooker, I cooked three-course meals. The third room was reserved for my chickens, though spiders of all shapes and sizes, and rats, moved in as well! The rats were later deterred by a cat, borrowed from my neighbour.

My daily routine varied, and depended on the clinic I was visiting. The longest trip was by bus to a place called Burie, where my day started at 5 a.m. and finished at 9 p.m. I travelled by local minibus and became well-known to the drivers. The other trips were usually on horseback and I could spend something like eight hours in the saddle (made from wood, but thankfully padded). This meant starting at 6 a.m., travelling four hours to the clinic, putting in a full day, and riding four hours back. During my travels I became known in the area as 'Mr George, the tall "Ferenge" (foreigner).'

Suddenly, and surprisingly, my time in Ethiopia was drawing to a close. Before I left, Haile Selassie visited the town as a 'peace offering' in the wake of the civil war. I used to be interested in cine photography, and had obtained permission to film the Emperor's visit to the local hospital. All went well until I felt a pair of strong arms move me gently to one side. Without thinking I apologized and carried on filming. It was only afterwards that a friend told me that I had nearly knocked over the Crown Prince himself.

Soon after this, unfortunately, I became ill, and had to return to the UK after only fifteen months of my projected two years. I had concentrated too much on my work, and had failed to look after myself properly. I was met at Heathrow by two VSO staff, and I told them 'I had failed.' 'We expected you home six months ago,' they said. In fact, I had not failed; and several years later, I returned to another part of Africa as a field officer, to continue the work of leprosy control which I had begun as a volunteer. I went to Ethiopia a young thirty-year-old. I returned a much more mature thirty-two-year-old. The words of my Chief Male Nurse at Moorhaven Hospital summed it up for me, 'You now know that the world isn't Royal Parade.'[1]

My particular project in Ethiopia was one of the casualties of the 1974 Revolution, which followed a severe famine in Wollow province. The work of leprosy control continues,

[1] Royal Parade is one of the main streets in Plymouth.

however, in the capital, and today, courses continue to be held in the Leprosorium for those involved in the recognition and treatment of leprosy. For me, VSO was not only a job, it was also an adventure in self-development and mutual understanding. Through my work with leprosy control, I came to know and respect a culture entirely different from my own. This respect has stayed with me ever since.

6

BOB SARGEANT. Born 1945, Leamington Spa, Warwickshire. He came to VSO in 1969 as an experienced pig farmer, and spent the next three years at the Catholic Mission in Alexishafen, Madang Province, Papau New Guinea, managing the Mission piggery and training local counterparts in the maintenance of agrigultural plant. Since returning to the UK in 1972, Bob has been a farmer in north Yorkshire.

I WENT to a meeting. The speaker had spent his holidays collecting beetles, or butterflies, in the highlands of New Guinea. He was fairly inoffensive, superficial and comfortably self-satisfied; he was dubious about the future of New Guinea. There was a man who went on an expedition rushing through other people's countries carrying a revolver and expecting obedience. He was on TV and in the newspapers. I don't think such people should be allowed out of the country; I would not tolerate him on my field here. Why should barefoot folk be expected to suffer him? And then there was a team of British potholers on TV; harmless but obsessed with their own narrow aims. They all went down with pek-pek wara – diarrhoea. They'd been eating rice, probably white, tinned food, and imitation jam made of boiled sweets. With proper planning or a bit of fair and sensible swapping they could have enjoyed all manner of good fruit and vegetables, and much better health. Chilli peppers can help to control the bugs in the gut which make pek-pek wara.

But then I decided *I* would go to Papua New Guinea, and I became involved with VSO. I remember some of the advice I received before I left England. A farmer who had spent many years as a pioneer in Canada had been told when he tried to grow crops and cultivate the land in the manner normal here, 'You're not in England now.' So I had to remember I was not in England and adapt to the local environment. I think it was Professor Bunting at the briefing course at Reading who repeated the old catch phrase: 'It ain't necessarily so,' and told us to remember it, and not make wrong assumptions. A lady on the course at White Hart Lane said, 'Respect women and their opinions wherever you find them, no matter how apparently simple, boring, or dirty the job they are doing.' Another speaker said that heavy objects could be carried in waistcoat pockets to avoid excess baggage payments. Fortunately it was before the days of hijackers, so the spanners in my pockets caused no problems beyond discomfort when I reached Port Moresby, and stepped out of the cool plane into the heat.

Journalists who are sure they have met cannibals in Papua New Guinea can be a source of irritation or amusement. The only time I was afraid of savages was outside the rear entrance of Oxford United football ground. Somewhat unnerved, I returned to college, where my African friends poured me a cup of tea and I felt better. The savage football fans were, of course, all white. In England increasing mechanization has created too much solitude on small farms. Work is less social than it was, and less social than in many other working environments. In Papua New Guinea I spoke to more people in a day than in most weeks in Yorkshire. And the warmer climate means that more of life is lived outside or on the veranda, and not behind the thick walls and closed doors of a cold climate.

But Papua New Guinea was not a tourist trap. It was a continuation of my life in Yorkshire, and a part of my education which has not left me. Whether it be ideas, plants, animals or buildings, development is about making things grow.

For me, development in Papua New Guinea was an extension of activities I had experienced on a smaller scale and as a lesser participant in Yorkshire. Lessons I learned and questions which I became aware of in New Guinea continue to influence my life and attitudes now, eleven years after I left there. The environment was vastly different, but enough of the work was familiar and people were kind, so that Alexishafen, or 'Sek' as it is locally and more conveniently known, soon became a second home. I was not unique in this last respect. Some of the teachers often found themselves almost adopted, so leaving was rather painful. A plantation foreman who had seen many volunteers come and go, explained that it was therefore necessary to drink a lot at the farewell party so as not to feel the pain on the morning of departure. It was not, however, as serious as a funeral, so he did not suggest using a special brew, known as 'Cognac', which was not alcohol, but stronger in effect than the brandy of that name, and never used except at funerals.

That first year was very full, with the welding of gates and the making of cattle grids, and my fortnight's holiday, which included walking with two colleagues to their home at Bundi, zig-zaging past obstacles and turning sixty miles by air into nearly ninety miles on the ground.

At 3.50 a.m. on the first of November, 1970, the big earthquake woke us all. At first I put my head under the pillow, and then I rushed outside. Everyone who could, got out, and then went back in and put some clothes on. There was much damage and many small injuries and narrow escapes in the district, but very few deaths, and none at Sek. Everyone pulled together to repair the damage.

One of my colleagues at Sek, Caspar, asked for my advice on a cattle project. This was not vital but I was able to help in some small ways. Initially, in February 1971, we inspected a piece of land belonging to another man only two or three hours' walk

48

from Darip plantation. The land was very steep, and if the trees had been removed to make pasture there would have been all sorts of problems, with scarcely a level spot for a cow to lie down. I think some of it had been gardened, for people garden slopes where they can reach up to plant taro and sweet potato and reach down to pick bananas. They leave tree roots and stumps, and that prevents landslips – except in an earthquake.

A fence had been planted of tiny trees, like a hedge, not just any old trees but breadfruit, cheace, and Galip nut. If they grew they would form a barrier and also help to feed the pigs in the disused garden. I was relieved when Casper eventually decided the land was unsuitable for cattle; it would have been very difficult to get anything going. I remember we found some figs growing on a small tree, beside the path.

Eventually Caspar decided he really did want some land of his own, where he could keep his cattle. As there was no land at Sek, Caspar had to move back to Aiome, his home village, along the Ramu valley. It was not a simple matter and it took several months to get things organized. However, with the help of the mission and the government, Caspar was able to begin. He tamed the heifers beautifully and I made some halters. I had said that the way people tamed pigs so that they were unafraid and obedient was much better than cowboy ranch-type methods. Caspar and his helper had those heifers eating salt out of their hands and following perfectly when led by halter. I also made a dehorning iron for use in a fire.

It was a big undertaking for Caspar and his wife. She was his brother's widow and already had one or two children, and now they also had a baby. They were leaving a regular wage, the convenience of being near hospital, school and store, and initially they had to depend on the gardens and produce of relatives. The last I heard, he had used his skills to save a sick cow or calf at the nearest mission. I hope he has succeeded in his venture.

Pat Ryan was an ex-lay missionary from Australia. He had managed the cattle department for some years but as he grew older his heart was not quite strong enough, so the doctors advised him to retire. He returned for a visit in August 1971 and brought the paperwork, which I had neglected, up to date. I seldom found much time to work in the office, except to prepare pay packets. On the few occasions I attempted it I could not keep awake, and had to go out and do something which did not involve sitting still. He also kept an eye on things, and met old friends, and enabled me to take a week's holiday.

On one of my trips to Bundi, Joseph Towse (a colleague of mine) and I were carrying toads to a village called Paita for a mutual friend Philip Arna. Paita takes its name from 'fighter', since it was the site of a wartime airfield close to the Ramu River. Brother Ben, our pilot, had re-arranged his schedule so that he could collect us from Bundi. The toads were destined to eat snakes' eggs, because the snakes can be particularly dangerous among the thick Kunai grass, and one of Philip's helpers had been killed by a snake. It had been fun collecting the toads in the piggery, helped by various people, including volunteers. One of them, Brian-the-bread-oven-builder, had a narrow escape when a sow's jaws snapped shut close behind him, and he nearly fell off the back of my motorbike with the box of toads.

Shortly before he went back to his village, Caspar taught me how to trap pigs, using light poles and sticks to make a trap which holds the pig without killing it. The clever use of levers was very impressive.

At that time we were unaware of the effects of leaching in the wet tropics. Pasture is not an adequate substitute for the climate's vegetation, which is Rain Forest. Kunai grass tends to grow and be maintained by fire, rather like heather on the Yorkshire moors. Neither are very good for the land.

Another colleague of mine was Martin Dai, a catechist and development worker, heavily involved in the Cargo Cult. In addition to his catechist's work, Martin developed his gardens and plantations to prove where the wealth really came from. He was a terrific worker, though only small and light, and a truly original thinker. Some years later I read

J. Sholto Douglas's *Forest Farming*, and thought it remarkable that Martin Dai had come up with similar ideas quite independently.

Coincidence: shortly before I left Yorkshire, a small Black Angus calf which had been hidden by its mother ran into some rough land. I pursued it and as I caught it we both ended up with a splash in a stream. Just to prove I was fit, I carried it on my shoulders all the way back home and my brother brought in the heifer, its mother. Some time in my second year at Sek a valuable white Brahman calf got under a fence and set off through the plantation. Eventually we caught it in the Bigs River, a shallow part fortunately. With a little help from my friends I carried it back to Jati Dairy.

Once, in late 1971, some friends and I were walking up a stream bed to bathe beneath a waterfall. Some of them were new to New Guinea, so I carried the cameras and was a bit impatient. I didn't bother to remove any shoes or clothes when I went in. At first, the air in my clothes supported me, but later I began to sink. I called for help and Christine from Wales and Patrick from the south of England grabbed me and brought me to the bank, where Helen from Australia helped to pull me out. It was a frightening but a beautiful experience.

Now a few brief thoughts of people who were there. Little Denise and her helpers who provided food even at odd times after journeys, and medicine and reassurance during malaria, and calm kindness throughout. Gina and her pigs. Andrew and his soya beans. Mike and his good humour and west country songs. Marie, who got us our raise to twenty dollars a month, one of countless nice Lancastrians I have met. I shall always remember Heather and the mother of one of her pupils practising Pidgin, making polite conversation while sitting on a dead cow, in the trailer on the journey back from Vidar. At Carol's send-off party at Rivo we ate the best pig I have ever tasted. It had lived on wild plants and nuts and fruit on a volcanic island. Carol could lead us in singing even more songs than Mike . . . and Sue, who helped me with writing about pig keeping, always patient and beautiful.

Joseph Towse is now working on Damp Plantation. He is not using any of the skills I taught him and they were of no use to him at Bundi. However, he has a wife and three children and he still takes photographs. Many adults in the tropics have lactose intolerance, so milk is no good to them. However, the dairy work did enable them to earn money and helped in the education of their children. There are many stories I have not told, but now it is spring and the sowing will not wait.

When considering the value of these activities, Schweitzer's yardstick is as good as any: 'Ask yourself the question, is it for life or is it for death?'

Em Tasol, lik lik tok bilong mi. Mi Bob Sargeant.[1]

7

JOHN WHELPTON. Born 1950, Nottingham. Joined VSO from University. From 1972 to 1974 he worked as a volunteer Lecturer in the English Language Training Team, Tribhuvan University, Kathmandu. He then spent six months as VSO's Assistant Field Officer in Nepal, evaluating potential volunteer projects. He then worked for the Ministry of Defence in London before starting postgraduate research work at the School of Oriental and African Studies, London University. He is currently doing fieldwork in India and Nepal for his PhD thesis, as well as co-editing the journal South Asia Research. *John's book,* Jang Bahadur in Europe *is due for publication in late 1983.*

ALTHOUGH I had earlier thought vaguely about becoming a volunteer, my actual decision to apply was not taken until

[1] Pidgin English: 'That's all from me. Bob Sargeant.'

half-way through my final year at university. By what turned out to be a stroke of good fortune, the Civil Service Commission had told me that they could not decide until later in the year whether they would offer me a job, and this news meant that I had to think again about what I was going to do after graduation. I applied to VSO, offering my services as a teacher of English, the obvious choice for a prospective classics graduate with an interest in languages but no technical or professional qualifications. As my preferred area of posting I gave the Indian sub-continent, attracted, I think, both by romantic images of India and by the prospect of working in a developing country where liberal democracy had a stronger hold than in other parts of the Third World. The post I was eventually offered was as a member of a team teaching in the constituent colleges of Nepal's Tribhuvan University, and so, in August 1972, accompanied by five other English teachers, an agriculturist and an horticulturist, I arrived in Kathmandu.

In 1972 there were fewer than twenty British volunteers in Nepal, the majority teaching English in colleges. VSO had no field officer, the in-country back-up being provided by the British Council, whose Assistant Representative had direct responsibility for volunteers. Training arrangements for new arrivals differed from year to year, and it had been decided that our group should train jointly with an incoming batch of American Peace Corps volunteers. These were going to teach English at school level and would in most cases be posted to remote hill villages, as much as two or three days on foot from the nearest motorable road or airstrip. These are, in fact the kind of circumstances in which many current VSOs in Nepal are working, but in 1972 most of us were destined for relatively soft billets in towns.

Nine weeks after arrival in Kathmandu, having completed my in-country language and skills training and enjoyed a fortnight's trekking in the shadow of Annapurna and Dhaulagiri, I moved to the Tarai town of Birgunj where I was to spend the winter teaching at Thakur Ram College. I rented an upstairs room, functionally furnished, in a house on the outskirts of town, about fifteen minutes by cycle from Thakur Ram, and settled into my new routine.

Birgunj itself is similar in appearance to many North Indian towns. Hindi and Bhojpuri (the latter is a local dialect found on both sides of the border) are heard more often than Nepali. Its commercial importance really dates from the early years of this century, when the Indian railway was extended to the town of Raxaul just two miles to the south. Since the 1950s Birgunj has been connected by road with Kathmandu, ending the necessity for travellers to cross the hills on foot. It is now the point at which most tourists coming by land enter Nepal, though during my five months' stay I was the only regular European resident out of a population of some fifteen thousand.

Life in Birgunj was thus a great contrast to Kathmandu, where the Anglo-American population was considerable. My main human contacts in Birgunj were my landlord's young son, who climbed up to my room most mornings for as extensive a conversation as my halting Nepali would allow, and my fellow members of staff at Thakur Ram, most of whom spoke fluent English. In the staff-room, however, conversation was normally in Hindi, many of the teachers being from India, so that I could only follow what was said if someone switched to English to speak directly to me. In a way I found this isolation almost enjoyable – it added to the sense of adventure. But at the same time it was a source of considerable frustration, and helped produce an almost obsessive desire to learn Nepali and Hindi well enough to overcome this barrier.

In addition to adjusting to a new environment, there was the job itself. My pupils were first- and second-year students, whose ages ranged from sixteen upwards and who were preparing for their Intermediate examination in Arts, Commerce or Science. The standard of this examination varied from subject to subject, but was generally slightly higher than British 'O' level, while the Bachelor's Degree, which those students who stayed on took at the end of their fourth year, could similarly be regarded as a little beyond 'A' level. The equivalent of the first degree of a British university was the

Nepali Master's, which could only be taken at Tribhuvan University's central campus in Kathmandu.

The English syllabus in the college had recently been reformed to put the emphasis directly on basic language skills, rather than on the study of literary texts. When volunteers were first brought into the colleges it was intended that they should demonstrate the teaching of the new syllabus for the benefit of members of staff who had themselves trained along traditional lines. This idea had, however, been abandoned, since most of the regular teachers had by now had some in-service training in new methods, even if the hearts of many of them were still with the old. I was thus going to function as an ordinary member of the English Department, whose job would be to teach 'Use of Dictionary' (in particular the phonetic transcription which the irrationality of English spelling makes necessary), to take the students through comprehension passages and grammatical exercises, and to improve their general conversational ability.

My initial nervousness gradually subsided as I got used to facing a class, but making myself fully understood was a problem which remained with me throughout the five months. Some of the students, particularly in the Arts faculty, simply did not have the command of English with which the schools were supposed to have provided them (but then, how many British schoolchildren, with five years of French behind them, could follow lessons conducted entirely in that language?). This was a problem other members of staff could overcome in part by explaining particularly complicated points in Hindi, an option which I obviously lacked. My difficulties were compounded because many of the better students could cope with English spoken with an Indian or Nepali accent, but not with a British one. I did come up against this on my initial visit to Birgunj during training: no one in the class I addressed seemed to understand the word 'wood' until the teacher who was accompanying me rendered it with a much looser pronunciation of the 'w' – the result sounding to my ears rather like 'u-ood'. Although the students became more used to my pronunciation with time, the difficulty was never completely overcome.

The system within which I was working also imposed great limitations. To start with, a syllabus which aimed to develop the students' skill in *using* English, rather than memorizing the critics' opinions on Shakespeare or Wordsworth, demanded much smaller classes than those at Thakur Ram, which could number up to one hundred. But classes were never reduced.

In addition, the great range of proficiencies within each class made it virtually impossible to plan a lesson which would benefit everybody. And at the most fundamental level, there were complications inherent in traditional Nepali (or rather Hindu) culture. The ethos of submission and respect for authority was, in some ways, a great help. I did not have to contend with the kind of discipline problems I would have anticipated with students of that age in Britain. At the same time, however, it reinforced an excessive emphasis on rote-learning, and on 'the truth' as something to be handed down from on high rather than sought out for oneself. Consequently, I spent a lot of time in class asking questions rather than lecturing. Having to do something more than just listen and copy down was a particular problem for many of the girls, since, with the interesting exception of the convent-educated, most were extremely shy in mixed company.

Because the work-load at Thakur Ram was light I tried to fill in my time with other activities. Most satisfying was the two hours a week I spent with an in-service group of school teachers at the College of Education. They were well-motivated and reasonably fluent, and I was able to concentrate on pronunciation problems. With a smaller class I could make proper use of the cassette recorder with which the British Council had provided me, and thus enable the teachers to hear their own performance. When I was originally introduced to the group by the visiting British Council Language Officer, he had told them how fortunate they were to have as an instructor a native speaker who, by definition, was incapable of making a mistake in pronunciation. This billing did not allow for the fact that, as a northerner, I pronounced some words differently from the 'Received Pronunciation' of southern England taken as a model in our textbooks. On one occasion I was nearly caught out by an alert teacher when, in writing a phonetic transcription on the blackboard, I gave the word (I think it was 'path') a short vowel sound, as in 'cat', rather than the long one (as in 'part') heard on the BBC and shown in the dictionary. I took the opportunity to explain some of the peculiarities of English as spoken by folk north of the Trent!

By the end of March, with the weather already becoming uncomfortably hot for my fanless room, I was quite ready for my scheduled move back to Kathmandu, where I was to teach for eighteen months at Amrit Science College – or Amrit Science Campus, as it was re-christened when the New Education Plan came into force later that year.

My work-load in Kathmandu was heavier than in Birgunj, but the pupils were considerably easier to teach. Science tends to attract the brightest and most conscientious students in Nepal, and Amrit took the cream of the applicants. Although for some lessons I still had to deal with very large numbers of students, for others they were broken down into 'sets' which were much more manageable. Having to repeat the same material several times each week could sometimes become tedious, but it did have the advantage that you could revise your presentation in the light of experience.

Nevertheless, there were problems, a major one being the internally marked examinations which were introduced under Nepal's New Education Plan. To ensure that marking was at least uniform within the college, I had suggested that each of us in the English Department should see all the scripts, but mark only one-third of the questions. My two colleagues preferred to split the scripts into three piles, each of which would be marked entirely by one person. That was therefore what we did. When it turned out that I had marked consistently higher than the other two, all the marks were allowed to stand rather than attempting some form of averaging out. This introduced difficulties over and above those produced by widespread cheating in exams.

My time at Amrit coincided with political unrest in the country generally. The *Singha Durbar* (Lion Palace), which housed the main government offices, was gutted by fire soon after my return to Kathmandu. Although the cause was never definitely established, it was widely believed to have been the work of opponents of the regime. The president of the Students' Union at Biratnagar Campus was later involved in hijacking a plane to India. There was also an attempt to assassinate King Birendra.

As elsewhere in Nepal, the student body at Amrit, or at least those of them who took an interest in politics, were divided into three groups: the Democrats, supporters of the Nepali Congress Party which had won a General Election in 1959 but had been removed from power the following year by King Mahendra; the Communists, of both pro-Moscow and pro-Peking varieties; and the Royalists, who supported the 'party-less Panchayat democracy' which Mahendra had set up. There was some friction between the various groups but politics at Amrit did not disrupt the smooth running of the college. In the years after I left that was to change: in 1979 a police attack on student demonstrators who had taken refuge in the Amrit hostel was one of the key events leading to the 1980 referendum on the constitution, and to some liberalization of 'Panchayat democracy'.

I did witness one very brief strike. It was on the simple issue of tuition fees at Amrit. During one of my lessons a crowd of students gathered in the grounds outside, evidently preparing to stage a protest march. The reactions of my class neatly illustrated the varying degrees of militancy in their ranks. Two of my students, both of them prominent in college politics, leapt up immediately and dashed out of the room. Several boys in the class then began asking me to dismiss them: they wanted to join their companions but were reluctant to defy my authority directly, or to miss part of the course. I said I intended to continue the lesson and that they must decide whether or not to stay. After some hesitation all the boys trooped out. The girls remained for a few minutes, looking progressively more bewildered, but eventually they too departed. This left me with a single pupil – the daughter of a member of the Indian aid mission in Kathmandu, who took no interest in Nepalese student politics. I tried to continue taking the 'class' for a few minutes, but was by now feeling very self-conscious as numerous students were standing at the windows watching the strange spectacle! So eventually I gave in and declared the lesson at an end.

The college was only five minutes' cycle ride away from my flat and my work left me with a lot of spare time. Apart from a few lessons on a commercial basis for well-heeled foreigners, I gave free lessons to any students willing to come to the flat. These included some from Amrit, and also friends who had regular jobs during the day and were studying in their spare time. I got used to the routine of rising at six, having a shower and breakfasting, and then teaching from seven o'clock until eight.

At a time when my work-load at Amrit was particularly low, a British Council representative put me in touch with a contract worker devising educational programmes for Radio Nepal, who asked me to script a schools' broadcast on the United Nations and its specialist agencies. My script was translated into Nepali and I was furnished with a copy of the finished product so that I could follow the programme when it went out two or three weeks later.

My spare time was passed in a variety of ways: reading, studying Nepali and Hindi, drinking 'raksi' (the potent local liquor) with friends, and cycling out to the temples of Swayambhunath and Pashupatinath, the most important of the Kathmandu Valley's many shrines. On one visit to Pashupatinath, the interior of which is strictly out of bounds to non-Hindus, I followed a young Nepali companion into what I thought was a complex of buildings separate from the main temple. On turning a corner I was surprised to find that we had in fact penetrated into the forbidden area. Since no one in the crowd had so far challenged me I decided to press on towards the centre of the courtyard and the inner shrine housing the 'shiva-lingam'. My luck ran out, however, and we ended up being interrogated by the local Inspector of Police. Eventually we were both released, the fact that my companion had declared himself the son of a senior police official in the Tarai (the area at the foot of the hills) possibly having speeded the process.

My time in Nepal was due to end in August 1974, but three months or so before that the British Council representative, who had been corresponding with VSO London on plans for enlarging and re-shaping the volunteer programme in Nepal, suggested that I stay on for three or four months to investigate possible new openings. Everyone felt that the college teaching project was not really satisfactory: it had drifted far away from its original purpose of demonstrating new teaching methods, and even where a college provided a reasonable framework within which to work, as at Amrit, volunteers were rarely fully employed. At the same time VSO was keen to shift the emphasis as much as possible to more directly development-orientated work, and to projects benefiting the least advantaged sections of society. Teaching students who often came from the better-off homes, and/or were learning non-vocational subjects, did not therefore rate a high priority.

Between August and November I made a number of fact-finding trips to different parts of the country, looking at potential areas of VSO involvement and checking on colleges to which currently serving volunteers might be assigned. As well as talking with Nepali Government officials in each district I visited, I saw a good cross-section of the work being done by other volunteer agencies – American, German, and Japanese – and by foreign aid projects generally. In my report I wrote that I saw the best prospects for future involvement in the extension of basic health services in the hills, and in vocational (particularly technical) education. The subsequent expansion of VSO's work in Nepal did not follow these lines precisely, since community water supply and forest conservation have been the major growth areas. Nonetheless, I had at least been able to provide some basic information to assist the first full-time VSO field officer, appointed a few months after I left, in the difficult task of getting new projects off the ground.

A description of one tour in eastern Nepal will illustrate my last few months in the country. My starting point was Biratnagar, the largest of the Tarai towns, and, by Nepalese standards, a major industrial centre. It was also the home town of B. P. Koirala, the Congress leader whom King Mahendra had removed in 1960, and it was still in many ways a Congress stronghold.

I visited the local campus, which was covered with posters denouncing the Indian Government's conversion of Sikkim from a semi-independent protectorate to an integral part of the Indian Union. Most Nepalese viewed this as an outright annexation and as a possible threat to their own independence, and all the different student factions had united on the issue. In view of the general political turbulence on the campus, the college Director said that it would be some time before Biratnagar became a suitable place for another volunteer. With this opinion I readily concurred.

While in Biratnagar I stayed with the staff of the clinic run by the Britain–Nepal Medical Trust, who were involved mainly in tuberculosis eradication. The doctor in charge had an idea for a 'Hill Drugs Scheme', supplying medicines at low cost direct to shopkeepers in the larger hill villages, and at the same time providing some basic instruction in their use. Some time later a VSO volunteer was in fact successfully employed in work of this kind.

I also met the Chief District Officer, a central government appointee with functions roughly equivalent to those of a prefect of a French department. Somewhat to my alarm, he promptly summoned a meeting of the 'nagar panchayat' (Town Council) for my benefit. The councillors included M. P. Koirala, brother of the Congress leader mentioned above and himself a former Prime Minister. After the introductions I had a general discussion on the needs of the area with the council chairman and one or two of his colleagues. They were particularly keen on securing a volunteer to re-plan the town's water and sewerage system – a major undertaking which called for a highly experienced engineer.

From Biratnagar I travelled north to the town of Dharan, at the foot of the hills, site of the British recruiting centre for Gurkha soldiers. VSO had placed a volunteer in the local campus two or three years previously, but her position had been difficult because of student resentment of the British base. The recruitment of Nepali nationals into the British army is disapproved of by many of the educated élite, though for the hill tribesmen who provide most of the recruits it is highly prized, both for its economic benefits and for its general prestige. Though successive governments make ritual opposition to the practice, they are unlikely to put a stop to it.

From Dharan it was an early morning start on the nine- or ten-hour walk to Dhankhuta, an extremely attractive hill town which was not to be connected by road to the plains until 1982. I stayed with a German volunteer and his Australian wife, met the Chief District Officer, interviewed some of the staff of the village industries training centre, and, with haunting songs in Gaelic issuing from the record player, discussed health problems with the Irish doctor running the Britain–Nepal Medical Trust clinic.

Two days of further trekking, including a thorough soaking from the monsoon's last fling, brought me to the hill town of Bhojpur; like Dhankhuta, both a commercial centre for the surrounding district and accessible only on foot or by helicopter. There, apart from allowing myself and my gear to dry out, I found that the local campus had enough work for a volunteer to be posted there next term. Two days later and I was on the long walk back to the Arun River and the grass landing-strip at Tumlin Taur. From there I was to return to Kathmandu by Royal Nepal Air Corporation 20-seater plane, passing over in a few minutes the ridges I had spent days climbing and descending.

In December 1974 it was finally time to return home, and the

New Year saw me behind a desk in the Ministry of Defence. Yet, in a way, I had never left Nepal. Much of my spare time was still taken up studying Nepali and Hindi, and my circle of friends in Britain now included a high proportion of people I had met during, or through, my time with VSO. I kept in close touch, too, with friends in Kathmandu and India. The following year a Nepali friend whom I had known since my teaching practice in 1972 came to the UK on a British Council scholarship, and the two of us worked together translating an account of the experiences of an earlier Nepali traveller, Prime Minister Jang Bahadur Rana, who had led a diplomatic mission to London in 1850.

Throughout this time I was becoming more and more unhappy in the Civil Service. In 1981 I finally took the plunge, resigning from the Ministry and enrolling at the London School of Oriental and African Studies to do a doctoral thesis on Jang Bahadur and the Nepali political system of his time, a system whose effects are still very much in evidence in present-day Nepal. I am spending the current academic year (1982–3) searching for material in Nepal and India, with the generous assistance of friends on both sides of the border. And so I come to be completing this account in a flat on the outskirts of Delhi, amidst the sounds outside of preparations for a traditional wedding feast, and with the road to Allahabad, Patna, and Kathmandu ahead of me.

8

CHARLES AND KATRINA McGHEE. Born 1952, Coatbridge, Glasgow (Charles), and 1953, Bellshil, Glasgow (Katrina). Before VSO, Charles worked as a News Sub-editor on BBC Radio Scotland. He was employed as a volunteer between 1977 and 1979, setting up New Nation *for Wantok Publications Inc, Boroko, Papua New Guinea. Charles' wife Katrina also worked as a volunteer for Wantok Publications, as Office Manager. After returning to the UK, Charles was Features Sub-editor in the Glasgow Evening Times, while Katrina became a secretary to the Independent Broadcasting Authority in Scotland. Both remain active in Third World affairs, Charles as a member of the Scottish Catholic International Aid Fund's Education and Promotions Committee.*

The call came the week before Christmas. 'I think we've found a posting for you and your wife,' said the girl from VSO London on the other end of the line; 'it's in Pee En Gee.' 'Where?' I asked as I strained to hear the faint voice above the afternoon buzz of the BBC's Scottish newsroom. 'PNG,' she answered, and then, realizing I'd never heard the abbreviation before, 'Papua New Guinea'.

Six weeks later, having given up our jobs, sold the house and car, stored the furniture, and bid a fond farewell to our family and friends, we left snowbound Scotland for the sunshine of our new home in the South Pacific. My colleagues at the BBC, where I had worked as a news sub-editor, gave us a rousing send-off, but, quietly, they shook their heads in bewilderment. My wife Katrina experienced a similar reaction at the office where she worked as a secretary.

We had made our decision, however, and as we stepped on to the plane at Edinburgh airport, after tearful goodbyes, we were sure we wouldn't regret it. The returned volunteers and would-be volunteers that we had met on our briefing course had fired us with enthusiasm. As we set out on that first leg of our journey to the other end of the world, a kaleidoscope of images flickered through our minds as we imagined life in this strange country about which we knew so little. In the short hectic spell before our departure we had been unable to unearth much up-to-date literature about Papua New Guinea. We were unable to counter, therefore, tales of cannibalism, tribal fighting and head-hunting in what one person described to us as 'the most primitive country on earth'. And although we knew we were going to work for a fledgling publishing company, our respective roles had still to be clearly defined.

We touched down at Port Moresby airport some two days later, having passed through a time warp of continent-hopping. The last leg of our journey from Brisbane to Port Moresby was spent in a weary daze. We listened attentively, however, to the Australian captain's broadcasts, eager to glean snippets about Papua New Guinea – but found we could hardly understand a word of his Queensland accent! The irony of the situation wasn't lost on us as we reflected on what the Papua New Guineans would make of our Scottish lilt. But we were here at last. We had volunteered our services, and now we were anxious to make the acquaintance of this new nation, then in its second year of independence.

Our first taste of the tropics was the blistering heat of the noon sun as we stepped off the plane at Jackson's Airport. It was a relief to reach the shade of the long, low terminal building where the VSO Field Officer and our new employers were waiting to meet us. International airports are bustling places, full of people hastily coming and going, the public address system constantly blaring. Jackson's Airport was strangely quiet, the silence punctuated by the low hum of the overhead fans and the occasional tannoy message. There were queues of local people waiting for flights. But they waited patiently and quietly, many of them sitting on the floor, surrounded it seemed by all their worldly goods (mostly contained in 'bilums', or stout string bags) and content to wait all day if necessary. We were later to praise this relaxed approach to the business of living, and equally to curse it, in the business of publishing.

Our base for the next two years was to be in the capital, Port Moresby, at the offices of Wantok Publications, publishers of a national weekly newspaper in Melanesian pidgin. In Papua New Guinea, 'wantok' is the pidgin name for a friend, relation, or someone from the same village or tribe who speaks the same language – 'one-talk'. There are over 700 different languages spoken in PNG; in the past, the country's hostile terrain meant that there was little or no contact between different communities, and even today Port Moresby is not linked to any other major town by road or rail – you have to fly or go by sea. As the country developed so too did pidgin, as the main lingua franca.

English, however, was adopted by the Government as the new nation's official language, and Wantok Publications were keen to start an English-language magazine, particularly aimed at young school 'push-outs' who had little or no chance of continuing their education. It was the brainchild of Fr Kevin Walcot, a former teacher and now head of the non-profit-making, Church-backed publishing company. He believed that a magazine in simple English would be of tremendous educational benefit to young people, ejected by a school system that didn't have enough places, but still struggling to master the adopted language of their country and hungry for information.

He had the idea. He even had a title for the publication, *New Nation*. Now all he needed was the personnel. Enter VSO. My brief was to examine the feasibility of producing such a magazine, design a format, plan its contents, examine means of production, launch and edit the publication. Katrina's role, in theory, was to take charge of general office administration. In practice she performed a multiplicity of tasks, from typesetting and paste-up to advertising and distribution. But for both of us, training local people was an essential element of the job.

We barely had time to form an impression of Port Moresby and its people before we were sent off to Goroka in the Highlands. Wantok had only recently moved its headquarters from Wewak in the north to Moresby in the south, and they were not quite ready to accommodate us. They also felt that living in the Highlands for a couple of months would give us a better insight into the real Papua New Guinea instead of the somewhat distorted image presented by the capital city.

Eager to embark on the task that lay ahead, we found the relative inactivity at Goroka frustrating at times. But later we agreed that it had been a good introduction to the country, its culture and its people, that would have been denied us had we never moved from Port Moresby. And we did manage to do some basic groundwork on the *New Nation* project, although divorced from the centre of our future operation.

We were stationed at the Communications Institute in Goroka, an audio-visual training centre run by the Catholic Church. While there we helped produce a slide series on the work of paramedics at small village aid posts, and a series of public service commercials for the local radio station. Our trips to the villages were fascinating. Despite the fact that we felt as if we were prying into people's private lives, the villagers welcomed us openly and the aid post orderly proudly showed us his little clinics which, sadly, were often ill-equipped and lacking essential supplies.

Two events, both of them co-incidentally connected with Church activities, served to illustrate to us at that time the difficulties we would face in the coming months in trying to bridge the cultural gap between our western ideas and the reality of life in Papua New Guinea.

The first was when one Sunday morning the priest in charge of the Communications Institute invited us to accompany him out into the bush where he had to say Mass for a small village community. Our destination was Bena Bena, an hour and a half's drive away along bumpy, dirt tracks which barely qualified for the title 'road'. When we arrived a group of people of all ages had already assembled on the side of a hill. The women sat in the shade, their ubiquitous bilums at their sides, picking lice from each other's hair. The men stood around surveying the scene. They were small, but fierce-looking, and many of them carried their bows.

There was a flurry of activity when the priest arrived. Some of the younger men helped prepare a makeshift altar. Empty beer bottles and tin cans graced the altar as vessels for flowers, the priest donned his vestments, and the Mass was under way, conducted throughout in pidgin. It was a strange, incongruous scene. We didn't understand that particular sermon on the mount, but the message was clear enough: we had a lot to learn about our new country and its people.

A few weeks later the culture gap was similarly highlighted when the then Archibishop of Canterbury, Dr Donald Coggan, visited the area to inaugurate a new Anglican church. Again we were invited to witness the ceremony, this time high up in the hills in a village called Watabung. The drive was much longer, the route more tortuous, as the Archbishop's entourage, transported by the latest technology on wheels, wound its way through a Stone Age setting where the way of life had changed little in centuries. The welcoming party included local priests and the village headmen, but the most colourful character of all was the churchwarden. I can recall the scene vividly: the Archbishop in dog collar and flowing crimson robe standing beside the warden, resplendent in his feathered head-dress, traditional nose-bone and shell decorations – and a red and navy striped 'school' tie attached to his bare neck!

I later helped a local journalist from the institute record an interview with the Archbishop and the talk went out on national radio. Shortly afterwards it was time to return to Port Moresby, and although we were anxious to get our project off the ground, it was with sadness that we said goodbye to our new friends. One of the local members of staff presented us with a bow and arrows which we still treasure. And just before we left, the wife of another staff member came rushing out, carrying her baby in her string bag, to wish us a tearful farewell. The language barrier that had prevented us from getting to know her well didn't prevent her from communicating her feelings. Would we be able to communicate as effectively in the task that lay ahead? It was a daunting thought.

Back in Port Moresby, we quickly settled into a small flat that had been allocated to us and set to work. Moresby was like an Australian provincial town, far removed in appearance from the village life we had recently witnessed. It had a large Australian population, too, most of whom worked in government service. And, of course, Papua New Guineans from all over the country – from the light-skinned Papuans to the rugged, dark Melanesians and the coal-black people of Bougainville. Europeans, Chinese and Filipinos added to the city's cosmopolitan image.

The next few weeks were a hectic round of meetings with youth groups, government departments, sports organizations, schools and printers, as we floated our ideas and sought feedback that would help finalize our plans for the magazine. We noted, in particular, that young people tended to buy glossy imported sports magazines and comics, and after much discussion with our colleagues at Wantok it was decided that that was the format with which we should be competing. The magazine was to be printed in two centres – a full-colour section in Hong Kong (because it couldn't be done locally) and the remainder of the printing in Port Moresby, where the two sections would also be collated and distributed.

Finally, in July, five months after we had arrived, all our preparations were complete. The material for our first issue had been collated. We typeset the features, and with the help and dedication of our artist Biliso Osake, prepared the magazine paste-up page by page at the Wantok offices before passing the camera-ready artwork to our printers. But there was no time to relax: we were already busy on the next issue when the first *New Nation* appeared in the shops in the first week of August.

From typing the first story to helping deliver copies of *New Nation* to the local newsagents, we had nursed the magazine all along the way, and at its launch the then Director of the Government's Office of Information, Mr Brian Amini, described *New Nation* as 'the most attractive package ever offered to the ordinary Papua New Guinean'. The first issue of 5,000 copies sold out within two weeks. The magazine went from strength to strength, putting on circulation month by month. Apart from individual subscriptions, *New Nation* was widely used as a teaching aid in schools. It was achieving nationwide penetration – from the main towns to the most remote islands. In our second year we even produced a special Pacific edition, circulating copies to principal nations of the South Pacific.

The road to success, however, wasn't a smooth one. It was *I hatwok long mekim* (hard work, difficult) as they say in pidgin. We encountered all sorts of obstacles along the way. When we first started work at Wantok, the total staff numbered no more than ten (half European, half Papua New Guinean). Space was at a premium in the small office and the situation was made even worse by unopened and half-opened packing cases which still littered the floor after Wantok's move from Wewak. It was a kind of comfortable chaos, however. Somehow the place didn't quite seem the same months later when a more orderly discipline had been established.

One of Katrina's first tasks was to learn how to operate the composing machine on which *Wantok* and *New Nation* were typeset. *Wantok*'s typesetter was due to leave shortly and it was imperative that Katrina mastered the machine so that she could, in the short term, typeset *New Nation* and, in the long term, train local people in the use of the composer. She achieved this quickly and successfully and we soon bought another composing machine and hired two local girls, whom she trained, to cope with our own work and outside work that we began to take in.

In the early days, while working on the plans for *New Nation*, my interest in photography came in useful when I helped establish a darkroom for the *Wantok* office and trained a young Papua New Guinean on the staff in the use of the enlarging equipment.

One of the most disappointing features of these early days

was the lack of co-operation we received from the PNG Education Department. Our publisher had been hopeful that they might co-fund the magazine project. He knew that they had had a similar project in mind for a number of years, but had never managed to get it off the ground. However, they declined to take part, ostensibly on the grounds that *New Nation* was a Church-backed scheme and therefore did not qualify for public funds.

We were worried, too, about the high cost of transporting the magazine all over the country – everything outside Port Moresby had to go by air. Would our income meet our expenditure? We had no option but to put our faith in advertising and go for maximum sales. When the artwork for our first issue was put on the plane for Hong Kong it left literally on a wing and a prayer. We couldn't afford a flop.

It was Chris Saulo, our young delivery boy-cum-darkroom technician, who was first to tell us that our faith had paid off. A few days after *New Nation* had first gone on sale, he came into the office grinning from ear to ear. 'They're all sold out,' he said. 'The shops want more *New Nations*. Right away.' He was promptly despatched to top up their supplies. Working and mixing with people from different parts of the country helped us to gauge reaction to how the magazine was developing and, of course, we were constantly guided by the bulging mailbags which never ceased to amaze us. Everyone, it seemed, wanted to write to *New Nation*.

Our early success, however, was tempered with criticism – mainly directed towards the glossy advertising and western comic strips, such as Tarzan. Even some VSOs in other parts of the country wrote to say how disappointed they had been with this aspect of the magazine. However, we needed the advertising to pay for our production costs (*New Nation* was not subsidized and had to become self-supporting), and we needed the strips to attract the readers who at present bought imported comics. The strips could be dispensed with later when the magazine was firmly established.

We felt that the positive aspects of the magazine outweighed these disadvantages and we sought to ensure that each issue of *New Nation* attempted to fulfil the aims we had set out for it: to help young people expand their knowledge of their own country and the world around them; to improve their general use and understanding of English; to increase their general knowledge; to educate them on topics of health, hygiene and nutrition; to encourage promising young writers and artists by publishing their work; and to provide a forum where young people could express their opinions and exchange ideas.

The *Wantok* staff continued to grow all the time we were there, but *New Nation* wasn't able to afford its own full-time journalists as yet. We shared *Wantok* resources and welcomed, on attachment, journalism students from the University of Papua New Guinea. In the field of journalism training, I also contributed to journalists' workshops run by the National Broadcasting Commission and inter-Church groups (the churches play a major developmental role in PNG, frequently acting in unison).

However, two years and fourteen issues after our arrival, and having more than doubled its circulation, the full potential of *New Nation* still had to be exploited. Further VSO support was sought and we were succeeded by another couple – Simon and Claire Swale. Simon, a graphic artist, and Claire, a journalist, were the ideal combination to carry on the work and helped firmly establish the magazine in the leading role it enjoys today.

Ours was not the typical volunteer experience. For a start, we were based in the capital city. We lived in a small flat with mains electricity, hot water, a telephone. We shopped in supermarkets and we had access to personal transport when required. Not for us the privations of life in the bush. Yet at times we felt isolated from the real Papua New Guinea. Our spell in Goroka and subsequent short visits to other parts of the country helped to compensate for this.

We made many good friends among the people with whom we lived and worked. Biliso Osake, our artist at Wantok, worked tirelessly for *New Nation*. His illustrations were superb. Through him and other Papua New Guinean friends and colleagues we were privileged to share in a colourful cultural experience. They introduced us to 'sing-sings' (displays of traditional dancing), 'mu-mus' ('feasts of food, cooked in hot stones), and invited us into their homes to meet their 'wantoks' and tell us tales of their customs and country. They sympathized with us when we were the victims of 'rascals', thieves who ransacked our home, and they made it hard to say goodbye when we were 'going finish'.

Incidentally, those scaremongers who had told us frightening tales, half in jest, before we left for PNG, were partly correct. There *were* tribal fights, particularly in the Highlands, but rarely of a serious nature (and not as frightening as the Brixton or Toxteth riots on our own doorstep). And there was one isolated case of cannibalism while we were there. Some villagers in part of the remote Western Province ate some of the flesh of one of their dead relatives – but as part of an ancient custom, believing they would inherit the qualities of their dead kinsman.

During our stay we were also privileged to meet and make friends with many other volunteers who passed through Port Moresby, and to play an active part in the running of the VSO Trust Fund. The volunteers in Papua New Guinea pool their salaries so that everyone is paid an equal amount. Excess funds are then used to support projects in need (*New Nation* was the recipient of a small grant).

For us, the volunteer experience was a two-way learning process. We received as much as we gave, if not a lot more. It gave us an insight into the third world and a continuing interest in its development, which is reflected today in our active membership of Third World support groups in Scotland. When we arrived back home we found it difficult to relate to our friends and families the total experience we had enjoyed. How do you explain in a few sentences or with a few photographs two years of your life spent in a completely different civilization? You don't. You've got to experience it for yourself, and it's an experience we wouldn't have missed for the world.

9

TESS PICKFORD. Born 1910, Preston, Lancashire. Before VSO, Tess worked as a journalist for the United Newspapers group. From 1977 to 1979 she was employed as a volunteer by the Solomon Islands Information Service, Honiara, where she was responsible for training journalists. Tess is now a freelance journalist; she has definitely not retired! A Group Scout leader, she was awarded the Silver Acorn by the Scout Association in 1982. Her ambition is to explore China.

MY GREY hairs were a definite asset when I started my job as a training officer with the Solomon Islands Information Service. The outward signs of my age won instant respect in a male-dominated society which accepted the experience of maturity. Otherwise, sex equality was nil; for generations women had done the work, while men languished in the shade of trees, doing the essential job of guarding the women against possible aggressors. A woman fetched the water, cooked, fed the children, worked the garden, did the housework. A man lolled under a leafy shelter, settling matters of importance with his peers. Walking to market with her garden produce, the woman carried a heavy basket on her head, nets of vegetables swaying from her shoulders, a baby at her breast, and two toddlers clinging to her skirts. Her man sauntered at the rear, his burden the bush knife to deter robbers.

Poor man. Perhaps I, in my own small way, was about to topple him from his privileged perch.

In these days of equal educational opportunities in the Solomon Islands, hard-working women are forging ahead, leaving men sitting on their vain backsides, wondering who-ever pushed them down. Against the odds, women are break-ing taboos which once ruled that anything connected with their bodies was vile – although in some remote areas women are still segregated during their menstrual periods, and a month after childbirth. In the islands' one town, Honiara, for example, some women have grasped the opportunity of an overseas education, have planted their feet on the first rungs of top government jobs, become a vital part of the country's medical service – and have their own football and basketball teams! With my western belief in sex equality, I dived headlong into this first flush of 'feminist development'.

As far as the men in the information office were concerned, it took a few weeks before I was accepted. I talked to them straight, determination tempered, I hoped, by native Lancashire humour. We blazed with rows, hooted with laughter, and eventually found mutual respect.

Our job was to issue news bulletins to the local broadcasting station, to the weekly government-sponsored paper (the *News Drum*), the islands' only independent paper (*Tok-Tok*), to the British, Australian, and New Zealand High Commissions, and any overseas agencies that were interested. We had to present the official viewpoint, something which I found hard to accept after a lifetime as a journalist used to freedom of the press. Not that the government ministries were usually heavy-handed with their bans – it was just that they could not be pinned down on even apparently minor issues of policy. The 'top dogs' were often quite approachable; it was the lower-grade, pettifogging civil servants who bore the greatest grudges. They all needed to assert their authority – and the buck stopped in our office.

My first battle was against a European civil servant. For the *News Drum* we had done a full feature on a new road across the island of Malaita. I checked details with the Australian engineer in charge of the project, and had the article vetted by the Clerk of Malaita Council and engineers at government level. Ten minutes after the feature appeared the office telephone jangled nervously. An indignant English voice demanded: 'What do you mean by "the road will be open in several weeks"? That statement gives an entirely wrong impression.' All work in the office ceased as I humbly replied:

'I'm sorry if we're wrong. When will the road be opened? In several years?'

'No, no, not so long,' he boomed.

'Several months?' I enquired mildly.

'No, before then.'

'Several days?'

'No, longer than that.'

I exploded: 'Then, for heaven's sake, man, it *must* be several weeks.' I banged down the phone. From that moment my office reputation was made. They were happy with a training officer who could meet civil servants on their own ground.

Maybe my temper became testy because of the appalling conditions in which we worked. Everyone agreed that our office was the hottest, dustiest, noisiest, and most over-crowded in the country. Built of wood, it was sited across the post-office car park, and it was always hazy with fumes from engines left roaring while their drivers spent half an hour in the air-conditioned cool of the post office. Choked with carbon monoxide, we were also stifled by heat, having only two small wall fans to stir the torrid atmosphere. Everything was filthy because of the clouds of dust which engulfed us from the unmade road at the other side of the building. So much for the 'island paradise' I had envisaged. It was more like the 'Hell Hole of Honiara'.

What a relief it was to escape from the office, by taking one or two trainees with me to work on a feature for *News Drum*. I aimed to encourage young reporters to think up ideas and sort out the questions they should ask, and at the actual interviews I would stand in the background, listening, so that eventually I could help them frame the article or, as a last resort, write it myself.

The trainees' greatest handicap was an overwhelming lack of self-confidence, especially in the company of Europeans. To help overcome this I often took the trainees with me to social events, but it was hard going. Despite the kind approach of most Europeans, many of the girls found it hard to mix. At the beginning, it was torture for them to interview a white person.

On one such occasion, as I led two of the girls to the posh Mendana Hotel to meet a former American general who had fought on Guadalcanal in the Second World War, I almost lost my personal battle. The girls stood rooted at the entrance, their eyes filled with fear.

'No, no,' cried Lily. 'White people are in there.'

'They won't let me in with bare feet,' said a hopeful Afu.

I kicked off my flip-flops: 'Wear these. They'll let me in. And remember, its *your* country; we whites are mere visitors.'

Lily was unconvinced: 'You don't know how we've been brought up,' she wailed, 'we've been taught to believe that white people are just below God.'

'Get in, don't be so soft,' I bullied.

And they did, being more afraid of my lashing tongue than the glories of the Mendana or the Yankee general.

Vicki, another trainee, had more confidence. A former 'Miss Solomon Islands', she was a beauty, a typical South Sea island princess, with a superb figure, beautiful eyes, and a warm, engaging personality. She was a natural as an interviewer, her good looks and charm giving her easy entrance to any society. But like most locals she found difficulty in writing colloquial English. Born on a small man-made island in a remote part of the country, she had learned one of the hundreds of local languages from her mother, picked up a smattering of English at primary school, and learned to speak and write it correctly at secondary school. But in a stilted manner, with no colour.

It was Vicki I took along to do a feature on Kakabona, a village only three miles from Honiara. It fascinated me because, close as it was to the capital, it was another world. The people went shopping in the town, listened to the radio about the outside world, but preferred to remain in their own village, with its cooling breezes, beautiful beach, and scrupulously swept ground surrounding the leaf huts. But, as Vicki reported, there were no labour-saving gadgets, and so it was hard work for such women as Elizabeth, mother of five, who in an interview explained: 'Every morning I am up early to get the family's breakfast – either rice or potatoes, with cabbage, and, in season, crabs (land crabs).' After her housework Elizabeth went to her garden, leaving her baby in the care of her ten-year-old daughter; children of that age in the Solomons are very capable of caring for younger members of the family.

Vicki's report continued: 'The mother works in the garden until she feels it is time to return home to feed the baby, and prepare the family's next meal, cooked either in a stone over the ground, or by steaming inside bamboo. Part of Elizabeth's daily routine includes washing clothes in the river, carrying water from the well, feeding the pigs, and bathing the babies. Hard work, but she says it makes the evenings more enjoyable, when, surrounded by her family, the young ones listen, open-mouthed, to the tales of the older folk.'

Elizabeth's peaceful evenings were only a hop, skip and jump from where I lived, in an apartment house known as 'the Pink Palace'. Our open louvres faced the G Club from which issued throbbing disco sounds, often until it was time for me to rise after a sleepless night.

Yet, to be fair, I also enjoyed some of the western world's leisure activities, such as dining out. We VSOs never missed the chance to indulge in the enjoyment of food and drink beyond the reaches of our spartan subsistence allowance. The Solomon Islands government paid our rent and rates, and supplied our cooking and lighting requirements. We had enough left for adequate, but not luxurious, living. That brought us into contact with the local people, who knew that, like themselves, we welcomed pay day.

Some of the more thoughtful, affluent expatriates, on fat government contracts, realized our meagre circumstances, and gave us regular invitations – hospitality of which we took full advantage. Our rapacious appetites were most noticeable at cocktail parties, where we moved from bar to kitchen door. That was the place to be stationed, armed with a full glass; we could descend on the trays of food as they made their entrance, and clear up the remnants before they returned to the kitchen.

The thirteen VSO volunteers in the country at that time were a good bunch; they were serious about work, witty of conversation, and managed to keep level-headed under some trying pressures. Our unofficial 'shop steward' was Paul, who was always ready to take the cudgel to the powers-that-be on our behalf. He was a New Zealander, a lawyer, who had been around the world, had lived rough, worked rough, and finally, while in Britain, joined VSO. I often told him that had I been forty – no, thirty-five years younger, I would have chased him. Not that I should have caught him, but it would have been fun trying!

Along with Paul was another VSO lawyer, David; as the only social welfare lawyers in the country they got an amazing variety of cases to defend: murder, incest, robbery; in magistrate's or high court, civil or divorce, their pleas were for people who understood little or nothing of the legal system. They also went to remote areas to explain the system to gatherings of local people, and made broadcasts in the widely spoken pidgin. They did a really valuable job.

Some of my trainee reporters went to the most interesting court cases, but such reporting needs care and experience, and I had to ask David or Paul to check before anything was published. One such suspect report was of a case in which a woman was charged with assaulting her husband. Admitting the offence, she pleaded that she had been provoked by her old man's unfaithfulness. Our reporter spared no details of the woman's lurid account of her man's many wanderings from the wedded path, culminating in the reason for the beating-up which landed her in court. Editing the story, I nearly choked as I read: 'I followed him to this woman's hut. He went inside and I could hear them talking together. But not for long. Then I heard bouts of intercourses. I got a thick stick, and when he came out I hit him over the head.' My trainees were learning about colourful reporting! But alas, such graphic descriptions could not be issued from a government office.

Other VSOs provided good news copy, too. Like the anthropologists Danny and David, who disappeared for weeks on end into the bush, returning to Honiara with sacks full of interesting finds. Then, in the museum, late into the night, they would ponder over heaps of bones, piecing them together in an attempt to add to the early story of man and beast.

There were engineers, agricultural and fisheries officers, librarians and teachers among us, all trying hard in our two years to pass on our particular skills to the Solomon Islanders. Yet I felt humble, with my meagre two years of experience, when I met church and social workers of various denominations who gave their entire lives in service.

Whatever the barriers of nationality, standing, colour, religion, or age, the common meeting-ground was Saturday morning market in Honiara. With the background of the sparkling, blue Pacific, and palms posing at photogenic angles, the market was a blaze of colourful, fresh produce. Piles of red tomatoes and peppers, heaps of yellow bananas, massive green beans, fresh watercress, shiny purple aubergines, luscious mangoes, sacks of ripening limes, sweet, sweet pineapples – all the fruits of the tropics – at ten cents a time. Between the rows of produce milled a happy crowd, all brightly garbed in their best to greet friends and acquaintances in this popular forum. The vendors came from outlying villages, enjoying their weekly trip to the bright lights to sell their produce. The younger women served from behind stalls fashioned from stone slabs; mothers suckled their babies, while toothless, pipe-smoking grans with sagging breasts held screaming toddlers under the market tap to give them a bath in pure cold water. The young men staggered through the crowd with bags of sweet potatoes, while dads and grandads sidled away to judge the merits of the various betel-nut stalls. In my homesickness for the Solomons I choke over the memory of the Saturday morning market.

By ten in the morning the market was too hot for European comfort. So, collecting snorkelling gear, we would pile into my Moke and go five miles along the coast to where the reef ran close to the shore. Only a few yards from the beach was another world – a magnificent kaleidoscope of floating colours; a marine wonderland where shoals of tiny fish of brilliant blue were chased by swanky fellows clad in striking orange and black; corals of delicate hue were a fairy playground for rainbow-hued tiddlers, and I could see it all – even with my one eye!

I knew the seas around Guadalcanal were infested with sharks, but of course it could never happen to me. It did. I was bathing with a group of friends in what was supposed to be a shark-free bay. Everyone had returned to the beach, while I lingered for a few more moments of delight. Idly I wondered why my friends were lining the waterside, gazing in my direction. Without specs, my one eye failed to see their gesticulations, and turning on my back, I cruised leisurely around the lagoon. One of the shore watchers swam out towards me – an elderly Australian who had lived for years in the Solomons. He swam smoothly, scarcely making a ripple, and as he drew close said quietly: 'I don't wish to alarm you, my dear, but there's a shark between us and the beach. Don't make any disturbance, and perhaps he'll not notice us.' I've never swum so quietly – or quickly. What made it worse, my hero had an arm missing. A war souvenir, but at that moment a horrific reminder of what could happen.

Funnily enough, age made no difference in my relationships with the other VSOs, all of whom were of a generation later than my own family, and only slightly older than my grandchildren. Perhaps it is true that shared experiences know no boundaries of age or class. As for the value of my work in Honiara, I now read reports by my former trainees in the newspapers which prove beyond a doubt that somebody, somewhere, taught them something. I can claim only the grass roots, but roots are important, are they not? At least I can claim that I instilled confidence into the girls: Afu has travelled overseas for further training, Lily is now an air hostess, and Vicki is giving her two babies a sound pre-school education. Perhaps I didn't waste those two years after all.

10

WENDY AND JEAN-PIERRE RICHARD. Born 1948, London (Wendy) and 1949, St Nazaire, France (Jean-Pierre). Before joining VSO, Wendy and Jean-Pierre both lectured in English at Tunis University. They were posted as volunteers to Nkrumah College, Zanzibar, Tanzania, between 1977 and 1979, where they worked in teacher-training and curriculum development. They now live and teach in France.

BY ALL standards Bi Sebtuu was a surprising Zanzibari lady. That a woman should have reached the important post of Senior Science Inspector for Zanzibar schools in what is still typically a male-oriented Muslim society is in itself quite remarkable. Her physical appearance was one of striking contrast: a pair of shrewd and penetrating eyes behind large owlish spectacles set rather strangely amid the folds of the long black veil with which every self-respecting married Zanzibari lady shrouds herself from head to foot. But then, by the time three of us were due to accompany her on a visit to a school on an outlying island, we had long since come to see such contrasts as a feature of life on the islands.

The events of that day in June 1979 are now fixed in my mind as summing up much of our experience. We left the Ministry of Education in a Land Rover early in the morning and enjoyed the twenty-mile drive up to the little port of Mkokotoni, where we were to meet the boat that would take us to Tumbatu before the heat of the day set in. The road winds up through the huge clove plantations which cover the hills on the western side of the island, and we searched the warm air for any lingering trace of the heady perfume of drying cloves which embalms the islands during the season. The villages of red earth houses were already awake. People were busy in the banana groves and cassava plots which prosper in the shade of the clove and coconut plantations, and the road was already bustling with the big yellow lorries and the wooden 'mammy-waggons' which constantly ferry people and goods around the island. Each time I travelled outside the town, I was overwhelmed by the beauty of the islands, by glimpses of the ever-present ocean and the constantly changing play of light amongst the trees. It made me acutely aware of my good fortune in spending two short years in such a place, sharing the lives and aspirations of the people who had adopted us so readily and warmly.

These feelings were in sharp contrast to those I had experienced on my arrival in the islands eighteen months earlier. At that time, Zanzibar had conjured up conflicting images of mystery and violence. I knew of the island's history as a slaving centre for East Africa, and that there had been a bloody revolution only thirteen years before, which had seen the overthrow of the Arab rulers and their British protectors. Fourteen thousand people were killed in one week, and many others had been expelled or had fled to the mainland, to Oman and elsewhere. After the revolution, the islands had been all but closed to western influence. We'd heard rumours of heavy policing, East German or even Chinese control, and of anti-western feeling running high. What we could glean in mainland Tanzania, where we spent several weeks before flying to the island, was not calculated to reassure us. We soon realized that people knew little of life in that part of their country. They tended to open their eyes wide with amazement: 'Are you really going to spend two years in such a place? They are religious fanatics. There's no electricity. Shortages of everything. They don't like foreigners. You'll be watched all the time . . .'

Plenty of rumours, but little first-hand information. The six of us who were posted to Zanzibar in 1977 were among the first group of Western Europeans to be invited to work in the islands since the upheaval. VSO reassured us that their contacts with the authorities had been very friendly and that they were confident that everything would be fine. They turned out to be right, of course, but on the day we arrived we were all more than a little apprehensive, and I remember anxiously surveying the scene at the airport with the crowds thronging the roof, trying to assess the attitudes of the officials for any signs of hostility. We quickly learned which of the rumours had been true (the least essential ones) and most of our fears were very rapidly allayed by the dignified but very warm welcome extended to us.

One of the advantages of living and working in such a small community is that the 'corridors of power' are very near to the ground. We met the Director of Education himself, who proceeded to explain the purpose of our work in Zanzibar. After the revolution, the English language had a very negative image, linked to all the injustices of the colonial period, and to the regime that had been swept away. Although the teaching of English was never officially abolished, it was tacitly discouraged, and much emphasis was placed on the building up of the national language, Swahili. The consequent decline in English had gone unchecked for ten years, although the medium of instruction in secondary schools was still English. This was partly because the only available textbooks were in English, and partly because in mainland Tanzania English was still taught. Island students took the same National exams as the mainlanders, and with their comparative performance growing steadily worse, a decision was reached to call in outside help to reinject some life into the subject. That was our mission. Three volunteers were to teach English at Fourth Form level in secondary schools, and three were to try to do something to tackle the problem at the level of teacher training. For the three of us at Nkrumah College the brief was an open one. It was entirely up to us to assess the size of the problem and then to take any initiative we thought fit. In the days following our arrival we were somewhat overwhelmed by the responsibilities placed on our shoulders.

We were glad to get down to work quickly: a few days later, the students returned from their holidays and we were thrown in at the deep end. My teaching was divided between a group of students preparing for their national exams, and two groups of

84

trainee teachers. The first group was made up of students coming straight from fourth year of secondary school for two years' training, while the second contained untrained teachers with five years of work experience, selected for in-service training.

We felt that before we could really begin to plan a course for the trainee teachers, we had to have a better idea of working conditions in schools. In the first month of our stay, the Department of Education arranged a series of visits to island schools so that we could see Zanzibari teaching in action. We were brought up with a jolt by what we saw, used as we were to the magnificently equipped European schools in which we had worked. The classes were usually huge: anything up to seventy children, often, in rural schools, sitting on a dirt floor, or two to a chair in the richer town schools. But the latter had sometimes been hastily installed in converted Arab palaces to cope with the enormous increase in the school population after the introduction of compulsory schooling up to Third Form level following the Revolution. In some cases, half the classroom was obscured by pillars, while other classes were installed in corridors or in huge vaults. The teachers had little or no material to back up their efforts: a piece of white chalk, a small blackboard and occasionally a couple of copies of an ancient and totally inappropriate colonial textbook. It rapidly became clear that few of the young teachers had any idea of what they were doing. Some showed great enthusiasm and inventiveness but too often the lesson consisted of endless repetitions of a sentence, or of the basic rules of grammar, or of incomprehensible dictations from some incomprehensible book. During one lesson a very young teacher managed to fill a whole forty-minute period for six-year-olds with various combinations of counting from one to ten, and jumping on the spot while repeating 'I am jumping'. His own English simply did not permit anything else, yet he was a dedicated teacher and in the months that followed became a good friend, often calling at our house in the evening to talk about his work. In another, more advanced class, the Inspector accompanying us felt compelled to bustle us out after ten excruciating minutes during which the teacher had tried to explain to his visibly baffled students the difference between 'some' and 'any', and had got every single example wrong. We lost count of the times we saw or heard that 'there are seven parts of speech in English'. The Director was right – something had to be done. But where should we begin?

Along with the Zanzibari counterpart assigned to work on the project with us, a Goan native English-speaker with many years experience of teaching at Primary level, we quickly decided that the only place to begin was the beginning. So we spent many afternoons, after finishing work at the College, in the relative cool of our friend's living room, writing a basic syllabus for primary schools which would give teachers guidance about *what* they should try to teach. Once that was done the next step was to distribute it to the schools. Here we hit upon our first problem: the Ministry had no duplicating paper. We went on a tour of all the offices in the building and had soon collected a huge pile of paper in all shades of yellow, including old circulars or exam papers printed on only one side. The stock we hunted out lasted us for the whole of our two years. It had to, for a few months later, in view of increasing financial difficulties, the Ministry adopted our idea and began to recycle its own paper. Soon our syllabus was ready for distribution, but what would the teachers do with it once they had it? Probably not very much. If we couldn't give them more help it would soon finish at the bottom of a cupboard, where the yellow pages would slowly turn brown. So we decided to withhold release of the syllabus while we worked on a series of teachers' notes to accompany it. We took the grammatical progression point by point, and tried to compile as many ideas as possible for the presentation and practice of each one. At the same time we made immediate use of the material with our trainee teachers, dividing them into small groups and getting them to 'teach' each other, using our suggestions. The first results were encouraging, with even those with the weakest English drawing strength from the realization that they could all of them manage to do something useful.

After a few months we felt sufficiently confident to 'spread the word' outside the confines of the College. With the Ministry, we organized an in-service course for untrained teachers during the first week of the April holiday. About fifty turned up, and we divided the time between periods of methodology, periods on the teaching of reading and writing in English, using visual aids, and sessions in the workshop producing simple teaching aids. By the second day we were well into our stride, and although the course was proving exhausting (eight hours teaching non-stop in the heat of the day), we were satisfied that it was being a useful experience both for us and for the teachers. Then, on the third day, we awoke to a strange and deathly silence. There was no traffic on the road outside our house. The Land Rover that usually called to take us into town did not appear, and we began to wonder what could have happened during the night. Eventually we learned that a cholera epidemic had broken out and that the town was sealed off. And so it remained for six weeks. We lived inside the five-mile limit which had been imposed, so we could still visit the other volunteers in town for the latest news. We could visit the deserted market in the hope of finding something other than green bananas, brought in by government lorries, but suddenly, after the bustle of our first months, we were plunged into a long and uncertain period of enforced rest. We knew that by observing the local rules of hygiene we had learned, we had little to fear personally, but we didn't feel too reassured when there was talk of turning the deserted boarding wing of the College into an isolation hospital. It was very unnerving to hear the ambulances with wailing sirens rattling up and down the quiet road. Most of our energy was directed towards surviving. We started gardening, growing spinach and tomatoes, and we learned to fish with a local trap, discovering the secrets of tides and currents. With the help of our neighbours we didn't go hungry – and we certainly had plenty of time to spend on the teachers' notes!

The epidemic was brilliantly handled by the authorities and

when, after six weeks the quarantine was lifted, the island suddenly sprang to life again and we all settled down to a long working spell from May to December. At the end of the year the College closed a week early to enable us to hold a second in-service course. We built on our experience in April, and spent a lot of time doing practical work in groups, as we did with the students at the College. We divided the work more efficiently too, so that we had rest periods during the day and weren't so exhausted. It was a happy and stimulating week.

By January 1979, after a year of work, the syllabus was ready and had fairly detailed notes accompanying the first three years of the course. In virtually every school on the island there was a teacher who had either just graduated from the College or who had attended one of our courses. During January we repeated our seminar for the benefit of teachers in town schools, and then the Ministry decided that the time had come to release the syllabus to the schools. We were to continue teaching at the College and working on the teachers' notes, but a proportion of our time was now to be spent visiting the schools on follow-up work. We first visited schools in and around the town, but getting farther afield was always a problem because the Ministry Land Rover was always needed for one thing or another. On a visit to Dar es Salaam, we'd noticed that VSO had a couple of ancient motorbikes in reserve. Eventually we persuaded the Field Office to send one over, and this gave us much greater freedom of movement. Visits to rural districts became an increasingly important part of our work. We would hold meetings with all the teachers of English in the school and then try to observe one or more teachers in action. This was not a problem since the teachers readily accepted that we were not there to inspect or judge them, but to offer any help that we could. It became part of our routine to take over the class and teach a demonstration lesson for the teachers, discussing it with them afterwards. We did this for the first time during the January seminar for town teachers. One of our 'students' on that course was the head of a school just next door to the building in which we were meeting. Towards the end of the week he approached us, saying that it all *sounded* very good, but that he thought that the teachers might gain a lot from a practical demonstration. He suggested that he might bring a couple of classes along for us to teach. The children duly arrived, smart in their navy and orange uniforms (each school receives cloth of distinctive colours), overawed by the large number of adults thronging the back of the room, and some terrified to see a 'Mzungu' (white) person in front of them. In Zanzibar mythology the Mzungu is the bogey-man who takes away naughty children, and this put us in a difficult position, to say the least! I remember vividly having an uphill struggle for the first ten minutes while the children tried to understand what was going on and I tried to put them at their ease. After a while both the children and I relaxed and came to forget the crowd, turning the lesson into a game as we asked each other questions using the objects and pictures and other materials. We all enjoyed it enormously. It was satisfying to discover that what we proposed really did work and the burst of applause from the teachers at the end showed that they had been convinced too. As a result, we had discovered the value of teaching demonstration lessons, coming into contact with real problems and talking them through with the teachers.

By the time we left Zanzibar in 1979 the programme was running smoothly, and it was with real regret that Jean-Pierre and I handed over the reins to our replacements. They were to continue producing the notes for the upper classes, although these wouldn't be issued to the schools for some time since the Ministry had decided that it would be wise for all teachers to concentrate on remedial work for the first year or so, a decision with which we wholeheartedly agreed. They were also going to work on the next phase of the project, which we all saw as training one of our exceptionally gifted students to take over the job of training her colleagues. This would enable VSO to withdraw gradually from the project.

Life on Zanzibar wasn't all work. Jean-Pierre and I had the extreme good fortune to live in a house on the College campus on a small promontory by the ocean, five miles outside the town of Zanzibar. From our windows we had a view out through the coconut groves to the sea, shimmering most of the year in the hot sun, with a fringe of uninhabited islands on the horizon. We rarely had electricity and on a hot summer's day we sometimes regretted that the huge ceiling fans remained tantalisingly still, but we quickly learned to cook on a kerosene stove and to work by the light of a hurricane lamp after sunset. Our fridge served as decoration for so long that we actually came to dislike ice-cold water!

Being surrounded by local people, we were forced to make rapid progress in Swahili. Our neighbours were mostly Makonde from mainland Tanzania and Mozambique, who had come to the island to work in the clove plantations, and had stayed on. They welcomed us warmly into the community. One old man milked his cow under our windows every dawn, and we awoke to find a bottle of fresh milk on the doorstep ready to be boiled for breakfast. Others provided us with bananas and cassava and gave advice and practical help when we were starting up our own garden, taught me to cook local food, and would often drop in for a chat in the evening. The neighbours' children took to visiting us because our house was, to them, an Aladdin's cave full of books, paper and paints, and they'd spend happy hours installed at the big table 'working' alongside us.

Every morning we were woken by the cry of the muezzin calling the students to the College mosque at six o'clock, and we'd rise to see figures flitting through the grey dawn between the hostel and the mosque. Sunset was marked by the same ritual, and our life took on the regular pace of the tropics. Our pleasures were plenty: exploring the coral rock pools at low tide for cowrie shells of all sizes and colours; working in the garden in the cool of the last hour before sunset; watering and weeding and watching anxiously to see which of the seeds from Europe would flourish in the climate. We took to collecting the cow dung around our house for our tomatoes, and the results were so successful that we soon had to be up earlier than ever to beat the neighbours to the morning's new stock! We learned the survival system of stocking up on goods which appeared in the shops, never knowing when they might vanish again, and then participating in exchanges with the neighbours so that somehow, miraculously, one always got rice or salt or sugar from somewhere. One morning a week either Jean-Pierre or I would take a couple of hours off work to go to market. It was pure joy to ride along the winding coast road with glimpses of the ocean between the trees and a welcome breeze in our face. We got to know all the corners of the market and usually managed to discover some special treat, some fruit or vegetable we'd never seen before. The market is a major social centre and invariably we met some acquaintance with whom to pass the time of day. Soon, people no longer turned their heads in surprise to see us go by on our bikes; we'd become a part of the scene and wherever we went in the island someone would recognize and greet us with shouts of 'Hello, teacher'. The students from the College took to visiting us too, to practise their English outside the classroom or to chart our progress in Swahili. In the early days we'd spent many hours sorting out the long abandoned College library, and now we'd go and open it in the afternoons so that the students had a place to work. Jean-Pierre ran a voluntary French class after school and was amazed by the students' enthusiasm and rapid progress.

In April 1979 we made a trip to Pemba, Zanzibar's lesser known sister island. Many of our students came from Pemba, and some had already returned to teach there, but it was our first contact, and what a wonderful time it was for us. We visited schools for a week and then ran our course for teachers, following this with a short holiday with other volunteers, themselves on leave in Zanzibar. During that week we were invited into the homes of students, we went to a wedding, received constant visitors bearing gifts of fruit and generally felt ourselves to be very honoured guests. How unfounded had been our fears on arrival, and how sad that mainland Tanzanians should still know so little of these beautiful and friendly islands which are now an integral part of their country.

And so we come back to that day in June and the trip to the

island of Tumbatu. With Bi Sebtuu we scrambled out of the Land Rover at the little port of Mkokotoni and sat on stones in the shade of the fish market while the accompanying official busied himself with our boat. This was the only trip we ever made where we actually needed official permits, but everything went very smoothly. We climbed into the boat, a fishing dhow equipped for the occasion with an outboard motor. For our part we would have preferred the infinitely slower but more picturesque sail, which remained frustratingly folded. The boat went fast and we were soon receiving great gushes of water thrown up by the bows. Bi Sebtuu fought to keep her glasses and her dignity, and we struggled to cover our papers and as much of ourselves as possible with a tiny triangle of plastic sheeting the boat owner had given us. It was to no avail, so we gave up the effort and relaxed to enjoy the rush of the air and the smell of salt, knowing that we'd dry out quickly on arrival. Or so we thought. We hadn't reckoned with it being high tide and with there being no moorings in the part of the island to which we were going. The boat stopped a few yards out from the cove, where the inhabitants, alerted by the noise of the engine, were already waiting. We all looked questioningly at each other. Bi Sebtuu took the decision. She took off her shoes, put them and her bag on her head, gathered up her veils with her free hand, and leapt into the sea. We followed, wading to the shore for a very dignified welcome. No one paid the slightest attention to the fact that we were dripping from our shoulders down. At the school we were fed on maize from the pupils' self-reliance plantations and then conducted, still dripping, into the classes. Not a snigger did we hear from the children, and what we saw soon led us to forget our dampness in a warm glow of enthusiasm and optimism. The young teacher did everything we could have hoped for, and when we took over the classes ourselves, all the pupils were obviously full of pride to show us what they knew. One of his colleagues had not yet been on a course, but the trained teacher had spent a lot of time explaining our approach to him. Together, in a tiny school in one of the remotest parts of Zanzibar, they were achieving remarkable results. The thing that delighted us most was the pleasure that both the teachers and pupils were getting from playing with the English language. A big step had been taken down a long path. We sat back and thoroughly enjoyed our soaking on the way back.

11

EWEN MACASKILL. Born 1951, Glasgow. Before VSO Ewen worked as a reporter on the Glasgow Herald, *being named Scotland's 'Young Journalist of the Year' in 1974. He applied to VSO in 1978, and spent the next two years as a volunteer Training Officer with the National Broadcasting Commission in Boroko, Papua New Guinea. Since his return, Ewen has worked for Reuters News Agency in London, and is currently a Sub-Editor on* The Scotsman. *Ewen's wife, Anne, worked as a volunteer Educational Programme Officer for the National Broadcasting Commission, and then returned to teaching mentally handicapped children in Scotland.*

GLASGOW AIRPORT on a cold, wet morning in January 1978. We are about to say goodbye to parents, brothers and sisters; small talk and silences as we wait for the announcement of the flight to London. Then kisses, a final hug, and two years begin to seem like a long time. At Heathrow, it is the turn of other volunteers, and we see the same scene re-enacted as they take leave of their parents before joining us in the queue for the flight to Hong Kong, the first leg of our journey to Papua New Guinea.

There is plenty of time between the processed meals, offers of 'duty free', and the compulsory film to reflect on the wisdom of swapping a happy life in Scotland for the unknown of Papua New Guinea. Aged twenty-six, I had been a newspaper reporter for four years and had loved the job: variety, interviews, by-lines, adrenalin pumping on big stories, good colleagues and good chat in the pubs. And plenty of spare time to indulge in climbing and walking in the Highlands. So why give it up? The main motive was a desire to travel, to see life outside Europe; but there was also a feeling that instead of writing about poverty and inequality it might be nice to try to do something about it, no matter how inconsequential that contribution might turn out to be. And there was Anne. We had been married a year: she was more idealistic, also keen on travel, and fed up with trying to teach anarchic children in Glasgow's East End.

We took the plunge and applied to VSO. We were not fully committed to the idea at that point, but wanted to see what VSO would come up with. After passing the selection committee we were offered posts in the Solomon Islands. We accepted, told family and friends we were leaving, and then received a letter saying the jobs had fallen through. We had almost given up the idea when another offer came through: I was to work in the newsroom and Anne in the education section of the National Broadcasting Commission of Papua New Guinea. We had reservations about the location, Port Moresby; a returned volunteer had told us that it was a violent place – but we decided to accept. It was about this time that we received an illustration of VSO's global outlook. A VSO official in London looking after us asked their accounts department to send us our medical expenses: the accounts department sent them to Blantyre, Malawi, instead of Blantyre, Scotland! We attended a briefing course in London a few weeks before our departure and were introduced to a new vocabulary – gamma globulin, primary industry, field officer, payback, wantok. Some of the talks were informative, some were not. We asked about snakes, the great fear of Westerners. 'Not to worry.' 'What about break-ins?' 'Mainly in Moresby.' 'But we're going to Moresby.' 'Not to worry.' Another Scots couple on the course, teachers who had handed in their resignations, received such a bleak picture of their postings that they decided not to go. Disappointing for them, but better to make the decision in London rather than in Papua New Guinea. For us, the best part of the course was meeting fellow volunteers and realizing that they had the same doubts and fears as we did.

I had read letters from volunteers in Papua New Guinea, spoken to returned volunteers, read the scanty and outdated literature and even met a Papua New Guinean on the briefing course, a man who warned me to watch out for a snake that looked like an empty beer bottle. But I still could not picture what the country would be like. PNG started to become a reality for me when we stepped on to the tarmac at Hong Kong and saw an Air Niugini plane with the ubiquitous bird of paradise painted on the fuselage. Naively, I had not imagined that a poor Third World country would have its own airline – especially a country that was supposed to be just emerging from the Stone Age. I caught my first glimpse of Moresby as we circled Jackson's Airport in the morning – rows of white houses surrounded by jungle, mountains and the deep blue of the Coral Sea. I stepped off the plane still wearing a jersey and the jacket I had put on in Glasgow, but the tremendous heat, even in the morning, ensured they were off before I was half way across the tarmac. My abiding memory of that first day was of what seemed to be hundreds of fans rotating uselessly overhead in the arrival hall.

I had half-expected volunteer life to be bush houses and primitive conditions. But that first day I discovered through jet-lagged eyes that not only did PNG have an airline, it had – or at least Moresby had – cafes, supermarkets, squash courts, swimming pools, high-rise hotels, and a yacht club. Somehow it was all a bit disappointing. Later, not much later, I discovered that the affluence was superficial, covering only the large Australian expatriate population and the very small élite of educated Papua New Guineans. There were shanty towns round the city centre and the gleaming white houses of the relatively wealthy were surrounded by high wire fences to keep the 'have nots' out. Some VSO officials, and many volunteers – those in the bush – maintained that Moresby was not a typical volunteer experience or that it was not the 'real' Papua New Guinea. But Moresby, with its ever increasing population and increasing problems, is very typical of the Third World and every bit as 'real' as the mythical 'hamlet in the bush'. In fact, though VSO maintained the image of volunteers connecting water supplies and advising on crops in rural areas, a high proportion of volunteers in PNG served in the towns.

On my third day in PNG, I reported for work at the news-room. Chris Rangatin, head of news and current affairs and known as the 'Black Buddha', told me I was a complete mystery to him. Not only Chris, but the whole newsroom, were mystified by my thick Glasgow accent, and any questions I asked were greeted with polite nods. A year later, however, I was being greeted by the young journalists in pure Glaswegian: 'Howzitgaun, mate.'

Radio in Papua New Guinea began mainly as a service for troops during the Second World War. Later, it was run by the Australian Broadcasting Commission, who set up an extensive network throughout the country and were largely responsible for the high standards and general professionalism. But the number of Papua New Guineans trained by the ABC was pitifully small. When independence was granted, the few Papua New Guinean journalists were promoted to senior posts in the newsroom, in other NBC departments, or with outside agencies. This left a big vacuum, which NBC quickly tried to fill. The news and current affairs department had about fifty journalists, most of them young and inexperienced. The news-room was lucky in the handful of senior men it had. Chris, the boss, a New Irelander, started in the days when there was still racial discrimination, and had taken a few knocks as a reporter. Boe Arua, the news editor, came from Hanabada, a village on stilts in the sea near Moresby. He combined his job with studies at university, and was continually dashing between the two. Francis Damien, a big, amiable Tolai, was the chief-of-staff, and ran the reporters in the same hard-bitten style beloved of Hollywood films about editors. Mark Auhova, from Kerema, was in charge of current affairs. The only expatriates, apart from myself, were an Australian, who had overall control of training, and an Englishwoman, who was chief sub-editor; both left about midway through my time there. I had the pleasure of being the last expatriate to work in a newsroom that had once been dominated by expatriates.

The NBC has had a crucial role in the development of PNG, particularly in trying to create a sense of unity in such a diverse country. A major problem was language: PNG has seven hundred distinct languages. This, allied to transport difficulties and illiteracy, limited the part newspapers and magazines could play in development, though *New Nation*, a magazine of high quality started by other VSOs, and *Wantok*, a Pidgin newspaper, were both successful.[1] But radio was the main source of information for most of the country: in remote areas, for instance, it was not uncommon to find children listening intently in their classrooms to schools' programmes, or groups of old men straining to catch a news bulletin. The NBC in Moresby broadcast throughout the country in English and Pidgin, with news bulletins from 6 o'clock in the morning through until midnight. The news was also sent by telex to nineteen provincial stations, where journalists added it to local news; this was then translated into various local languages (or as many as the stations could handle, usually about five or six).

Most of my work for NBC consisted of organizing training courses, checking the stories of young journalists, writing a monthly newsletter/instruction sheet, and visiting provincial stations. With only four years' experience behind me, I was hardly dripping with pearls of wisdom about journalism; but I hammered away at the need for clear English, objectivity, and the avoidance of libel. Many had done a one-year course in journalism at university, where they had been taught by an able New Zealand journalist, and had already mastered the basics of the trade. I worked with the Australian training officer on a little booklet for NBC journalists; some of it contained good advice, but on reflection much of it was irrelevant, full of

[1] See Chapter Nine by Charles McGhee.

grammatical niceties that are not adhered to even in Fleet Street. The old adage is that journalists are born, not made, and there is much truth in this. The best of the young Papua New Guineans pushed to the top through their own enthusiasm: John Eggins, a Highlander, who tackled the difficult subject of tribal fighting and made an award-winning documentary; Newman Cuthbert, who returned from a spell with the BBC in London elocuting rather than speaking; Weni Moka, sharp, and honest, who demonstrated the absence of sexual discrimination in PNG; and Bunam Lakasa, an indisciplined reporter but a good sub-editor. The training was seldom in the classroom, but mainly on the job, dealing with live stories. I got breaks from training when others were ill and I had to fill in as news editor, chief-of-staff and sub-editor. The chief sub-editor's job involved starting at 4 a.m. and preparing a ten-minute bulletin for 6 a.m., a constant fight against the clock. One morning the clock in the newsroom was five minutes slow and I turned on the radio to hear the announcer say he was waiting for the news to arrive. Even 'training' officers are fallible!

I spent a particularly enjoyable spell reporting in the Highlands, based at Goroka. Arriving from the heat of Moresby to the permanent spring of the Highlands was a cool awakening: it was great just to feel cold again. People were incredibly open and it was not difficult to dig up stories. On one trip, I went with a recording crew high into the mountains for the opening of a new school. Sitting in the village, I could hear people from other villages singing and yodelling on the distant ridges long before they arrived for the feast. The ceremony did not begin until hours after it should have; the speeches were too long, but who was worried about time? The feasting, singing and dancing went on late into the night. No one seemed to find the presence of a white man strange. Being part of NBC helped: in other areas, while driving NBC vans, people would invariably wave. It was nice to be part of a popular institution.

It was also while I was in Goroka that I covered a road accident in which seven people died. The driving in Papua

New Guinea was reckless, but nowhere more so than on the Highlands Highway. I quoted the Police Chief as saying the driver had taken the bend too fast, and for me that was the end of the story. But for the local population the 'real' story was that black magicians were responsible. It is easy to be patronizing about black magic, but in PNG it is potent. Apart from the psychological power, black magicians use poison. For me, it was just an accident: for the local population it was all tied up with previous events, black magic, and 'payback', the ruthless PNG version of an 'eye for an eye'. Goroka itself was an amazing place: I saw a warrior in Highland dress, ignoring the laws about carrying bow and arrows inside the town boundary, standing outside a shop window full of fridges and washing machines – a startling contrast between old and new.

Anne worked in NBC's education department, writing scripts for schools' broadcasting. She wrote a lot of original material, as well as dramatizing books. She even acted in and produced some of the programmes. One series she wrote was on folk-tales. Naturally most of these were from Papua New Guinea, but when that supply was exhausted it was supplemented by the best known of the European stories, and eventually even a couple of Scottish ones. I wonder what the children made of 'The Fairy Flag of Dunvegan'. Her boss was John Billy Tokume, a celebrity in PNG for his broadcasts, his acting and his banter while playing softball, a game imported from the USA.

The expatriate population, including volunteers, often criticized the standards of NBC. A classic incident that was always mentioned was that of the quizmaster who asked who was the Queen of Papua New Guinea. The boy replied that she was Queen Elizabeth II. The quizmaster said that that was incorrect; it was Queen Elizabeth the Eleventh. That was a howler, but it was the exception rather than the rule, and I can think of bigger howlers from the British press and radio. Expatriates also found the standard of English poor, forgetting that for some of the journalists and announcers English was not just a second language, but sometimes a third or fourth. And anyway, it was for Papua New Guineans, not expatriates, that they were broadcasting.

In my first few months in PNG, I suffered from home-sickness, and began ticking off the days in the calendar until we would return to Scotland. But this feeling, common to many volunteers, soon passed. Scotland were playing in the World Cup in Argentina that first year and I got up at 6 a.m. to tune into the BBC World Service commentaries on the games. When I heard the results I was glad to be in PNG, but even there I had to put up with taunts from Sassenach volunteers.

Our flat, provided by the NBC, was a quarter of a mile from the studios, but at midday even walking that short distance would leave us dripping with sweat. The block of flats was of a garish design, a mixture of traditional paintings in loud colours and metal grills and fences; a cross between Disneyland and Alcatraz, that most people, even long-term residents of Moresby, assumed was a museum or art gallery. It was built by an Irishman. In comparison with volunteers in the bush, the flat was luxurious – a shower, electricity and a cooker. We shared the flat with geckos, the cheerful little lizards that can run up walls and across ceilings and are supposed to be good luck. There were also the inevitable cockroaches: Anne's brother is a sanitary inspector and had supplied us with enough poison to knock out a herd of elephants, but it had little impact on the cockroaches. We also had a baby snake in our kitchen, which I misguidedly chased around in my bare feet. The block of flats was small, but it contained Papua New Guineans, Filipinos, New Zealanders and Australians; and the cooking smells, general chatter and music were never boring.

There were more than a dozen VSOs in Moresby, plus volunteers from Canada and Australia. VSO warned at the briefing course against becoming involved in a volunteer clique, but it would have been unnatural for the volunteers in Moresby to have ignored one another. The ties of friendship among the volunteers were strong, but it was never a clique; almost all the Moresby VSOs were involved in Papua New Guinean social life, from playing in local cricket clubs to acting

100

with the local theatre group. The closest thing to a clique was the volunteer football side, but even then half the team were Papua New Guinean. The sense of camaraderie among the volunteers throughout the country was high; I travelled to various parts of the country and wherever there was a volunteer I was invariably offered a place to stay. We still keep in touch with many of the friends we made in PNG, though they are scattered all over the UK and abroad. VSO staff sometimes said PNG was a soft option, and in some ways it was. There was no language difficulty, there was no real bitterness against whites because PNG's colonial experience was remarkably short and only touched a small part of the country. The pay was higher than in other countries, the country was comparatively rich in natural resources, and only had a population of three million. Perhaps that is why so many volunteers stayed on after their two years were up.

Charles and Katrina McGhee, Scots volunteers also based in Moresby, became close friends. They were responsible for setting up *New Nation*, now the best-selling magazine in the Pacific. Charles had worked with the BBC before going to PNG; it always seemed ironic to me that a radio man should be working for the press, while a newspaperman was working for radio.

I found I was very accident-prone in PNG. At home I had been involved in mountaineering, but only once in ten years could I recall ever being in a dangerous situation, and even that was kept well under control. But in PNG it was just one thing after another. I gave a pint of blood, fainted, split my head and needed stitches; I fell into the fast-flowing Goldie River; I was caught in a savage current while swimming close to the beach; a car I was driving was smashed by a dumper truck; I had a fever that knocked me on my back for a fortnight – the hospital could not confirm what it was as they had run out of slides for taking blood samples; I was badly stung by a version of a Portuguese man-of-war – a doctor said, 'Is your breathing OK? Good: it won't be fatal this time.' PNG was a dangerous place. One incident in particular sticks out, though in this case I was happy to be an observer. After a football match, both sides jumped into the nearest river. I had come out early and was sitting on the bank when a death adder was spotted swimming down the side of the river. Snakes are supposed to be non-aggressive, but this one darted in the direction of the swimmers. Among the swimmers was a former volunteer, Denis Calderon, who had a healthy aversion to snakes as he had already been bitten by a Papuan Black, one of the most deadly snakes in the world. He was suffering from cramp and was being accompanied by volunteers as he swam back to the bank when the shout went up 'Death adder'. A potentially ugly situation was defused when a lemonade bottle was thrown at the snake and it changed direction.

I am not sure what the NBC got from my time with them, but I learned much from the experience. Attitudes I had adopted in Britain, like guarding freedom of the press at all costs, had to be adjusted to accommodate the realities of a developing country. Freedom of the press had to be exercised in a much more responsible way than in the West. Western-style 'conflict' journalism, where issues are polarized and differences rather than common ground emphasized, are not appropriate to a developing country. I tried to avoid becoming involved in policy issues for that reason: better to let the Papua New Guineans choose their own road without interference by a Western-orientated journalist. I had enough to do anyway looking after the basics of journalism. One exception was when a Government Minister tried to 'discourage' NBC journalists from covering a court case involving another Minister. In the West, this would have been a major political scandal. I was all for broadcasting an account of what seemed to be a blatant attempt to inferfere with press freedom. The decision rested with Chris and the other members of NBC's executive, and they decided to broadcast, a move which greatly embarrassed the Government. On reflection, perhaps a quiet word in the Minister's ear might have been a better approach, rammed home by giving prominent coverage to the court case he was so keen to keep off the air.

The NBC was always walking a tightrope. The Prime Minister made many scathing attacks on the newsroom, and since the Government held the purse strings this could make life awkward. It was difficult to walk the middle ground between being a Government propaganda machine and having total freedom, but the senior newsmen did their best. At times this could be traumatic, and the NBC no doubt has many more difficult times ahead.

In the hall of our house in Edinburgh there is a three-foot high copper 'beating' with the kundu drum motif of the NBC and an inscription round the side from the NBC staff. It was commissioned from the art school as a farewell present and is one of the proudest possessions we have. It was presented at a farewell feast at Chris's house, a traditional 'mu-mu', in which chicken is covered with coconut milk, wrapped in banana leaves, and cooked on hot stones buried in a hole – delicious! The copper beating is the only tangible thing we took from Papua New Guinea. But we also took a host of great memories, of an exciting two years among good people and good friends.

A warm morning in November 1979 at Jackson's airport. NBC staff arrived to see us off along with volunteers. Perhaps not the same sadness we felt when we left Glasgow, but a sadness nevertheless at leaving so many friends behind. Two years had gone by very quickly.

12

FELICITY BREET. Born 1953, Billingham-on-Tees, Cleve-land. Taught in a number of schools in Halifax, Harlow and Hertfordshire before applying to VSO in 1978. From 1978 to 1980 she worked as a volunteer English teacher at the Govern-ment Teacher's College, Doko, Niger state, Nigeria. She is now a Lecturer in English at the College of Education, Sokoto State, Nigeria.

ARRIVING at the VSO Field Office, Kaduna, in September 1978 was a surprisingly pleasant experience. The sticky heat, smoothing the sun's path into my first tropical day, the brilliantly coloured flowers, the romantic mosquito nets, and the spotlessly clean guest-room made me feel as if life in Nigeria might not be as difficult as I had thought.

I left Kaduna for Minna, feeling exhilarated. The journey did dull my glittering optimism a little, but once I had settled into the main hotel (after the usual differences of opinion) I felt as if I was on holiday. The Ministry of Education is, however, not a holiday experience, and I was glad that after only a week I was declared 'processed' by the Ministry and 'regularized' by the Immigration Office.

As luck would have it, the Principal of my project was in Minna for a meeting. He sent a message to me: we would leave for Doko tomorrow. This was the end of the holiday feeling. Instead, I was filled with anger and terror as I sat inside my mosquito net wondering what I was doing there. I reviewed all my reasons for becoming a volunteer. What had sounded dynamic and noble in St Albans now sounded empty and pathetic. I resolved to go home in the morning, and fell asleep.

As I woke up, I realized that I couldn't go home yet, partly because giving up without a struggle is not my way, but also because I knew I wouldn't be able to face my family and friends

Chris Tipple, one of VSO's first eight volunteers, teaching English
at Akropong, Ghana.

The 'cup winners' from Kolenten, coached by Joe Ogden in
Kambia, Sierra Leone, 1966-7.

Changing fashions? A group of volunteers about to fly out to Sierra
Leone in 1968.

A street scene in Birgunj, Nepal, where John Whelpton
spent two years teaching in the
English-as-a-Foreign-Language Unit, at Tribhuvan University.

Two faces of librarianship in Africa. Ivy Hill with a mobile library on the Chadiza Road, Eastern Province, Zambia; and training library assistants at Wesley College, Kumasi, Ghana.

Working for a 'New Nation': Charles and Katrina McGhee with artist Bisilo Osake, preparing an edition of *New Nation* for Wantok Publications, in Papua New Guinea.

Special education projects represent a small but important part of VSO's overseas programme. Like Anna Szuminska in Sarawak, Carol Williams in Kenya works with mentally handicapped children, using basic agriculture to improve their motor and other skills.

John Meikle and Sylvia Galvin with some of the pupils at the Beth Torrey Home for the Mentally and Physically Handicapped, in Nigeria.

In his essay on brick-making in the Sudan, Colin Grieg stresses the vital developmental importance of using local resources to make strong and reliable building materials. Better bricks make better schools, health centres and houses. Shown here and overleaf are two views of the brick works near Juba where Colin is training local counterparts in brick-making techniques.

The essence of volunteering lies in working and learning together. Here Ernie Shimmin and a local counterpart share a thorny problem on the Soy Appropriate Implements Project in Kenya.

Mechanics and electronics training is another important aspect of technical development. Brian Robertson is seen here instructing in the intricacies of fridge compressors, at the Radio and Electronics Laboratory in Colombo, Sri Lanka.

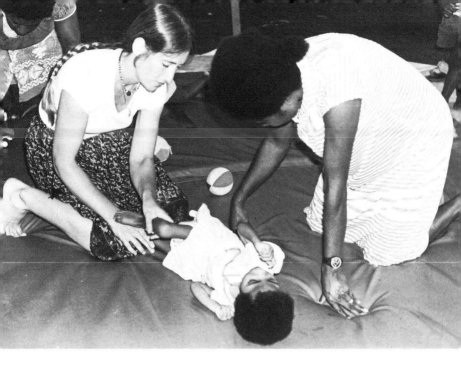

Around 10% of VSO volunteers work in health care, as
doctors, nurses, midwives, dentists, lab technicians,
physiotherapists and occupational therapists. Angela
Edwards worked for two years in Lae, Papua New Guinea,
as a volunteer physiotherapist. She and her counterpart are
seen here working with a five-year-old child with cerebral palsy.

Getting plastered! Tricia Baker also worked as a VSO
physiotherapist, this time for the Cheshire Homes in
Southern Sudan.

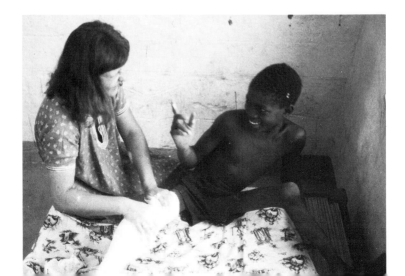

VSO health projects lay particular emphasis on the value of primary, preventive health care. Rebecca Scott spent two years working with Bangledeshi paramedics at 'Gono Unnayan Prochesta'—the 'People's Development Efforts'. In this picture she is showing a local health worker how to clean syringes.

Linda Manning holding an impromptu clinic on the road to
Ikumdi, Papua New Guinea.

In Dhaka, Bangladesh, VSO volunteer Pat Walsh is working for the Centre for the Rehabilitation of the Paralysed. One of the techniques she uses is to work with her patients on manufacturing toys and other artefacts, such as the doll shown in this picture.

Over 40% of all VSO volunteers work in formal education—in secondary teaching, primary and secondary teacher-training, librarianship and curriculum development. Felicity Breet, Wendy and Jean-Pierre Richard, Julie Bartrop and others in this book all worked in similar circumstances to Pamela Powell, shown here teaching in a Zambian classroom.

Efficient printing is vital to any developing country
wishing to improve and expand its educational system.
Greg Swann is seen here training Nepalis in basic printing
technology at Tribhuvan University, Kiritipur.

'Food first' is a common saying in development circles. With an estimated 800 million people in developing countries living in 'absolute poverty', the need for more food, of the right kind, and more equitably distributed, is clearer than ever. VSO makes a small but significant contribution to this end by sending over 140 agricultural volunteers to the Third World every year. Shown above is Paul Hitchman's project in Anandpura, Sri Lanka.

VSO's overall aim in its agricultural programme is to increase the self-reliance of local farmers. Here in Bugcaon, in the Philippines, small-scale farmers have set up a co-operative to improve production in the face of competition from multi-national companies buying up land around them.

Jill and Henry Neusinger's speciality is experimental dry-zone farming. In Udawelayagama, Sri Lanka, they are trying out new ideas and new techniques to improve local food production. The Neusingers are seen here with local villagers working on their experimental fish tanks and chicken-coops.

Learning starts early! John Young, VSO agriculturist engaged in farm survey work, is seen here discussing results with a Sri Lankan youngster at Gami Seva Sevana, Galaha.

in Britain. I had left for two years; I could hardly go back after two weeks. Not the most positive way to set off on possibly the most important journey of my life, but it did satisfy me at the time.

My college Principal, a small bespectacled man in a suit, arrived promptly in his big blue car. We packed my two cases into the boot, and I said goodbye to the other volunteers (half sadly, half proudly) as we drove off. At last I was on my way to 'My Project'.

The road from Minna to Bida is tarred, but very narrow. We pulled over several times to allow oncoming vehicles to pass, and once we had to leave the road altogether as a huge 'mammy-wagon' (a small taxi-cum-bus) refused to move over at all. Names which now seem more familiar than Carlisle or Watford Gap appeared – Zungeru, Wushishi, Lemu, and then, at last, Bida.

I had read the description of my project many times. I knew that we were now only about fifteen miles from Doko, so we were almost there. Of course, at the time, I didn't know what 'a difficult road' was, and looking back now, when most of it is tarred, I can only remember the outstanding details. It was a narrow laterite and sand track running through guinea corn which towered over the car like triffids. As we skidded and bumped along in the sand, I wondered where all the people were. Later I met hundreds of people on that road, but on that September day I am convinced that the road was completely deserted.

At last a sign appeared, 'Government Teachers' College, Doko, 3km'. The sun was low in the sky and my heart was low in my boots as we bounced towards the College. As we approached the main gate, I gasped in surprise, 'Oh, a luxury coach, does it belong to the College?'

'Yes.'

'Can anyone arrange to use it?'

'No.'

A long silence followed while I decided whether or not to continue. 'Perhaps I'll be able to use it next year, when I've had time to really become part of GTC Doko?'

'Ms Breet, I don't think you will. It broke down the day it arrived. Something spoiled in the back axle and the spare part has to come from Brazil. We've been waiting for it to arrive for two years. No one has ever used the bus.' There wasn't very much I could say in reply, so I made a non-committal noise and looked out of the window.

I knew that there had been six hundred 'pivotal students' at Doko last year. Most had left secondary schools without suitable qualifications and enrolled here for a two-year intensive Primary Teachers' course. Even though it was evening, I had expected to see a few students here and there. But wherever I looked, all I could see was empty space, empty chairs – where was I? Where were they? What was I doing in this hot, isolated, deserted place?

The big blue car pulled up beside a large, bright orange bungalow with a garage full of chickens. I sat still, looking carefully at the other houses. They all looked inhabited, but still I couldn't see another human being. 'This house is for you,' the Principal grunted, as he dragged my heavy suitcase up the front step. 'Wait, I will bring the key.' I sat down on the dusty step watching the dusk deepen. Such a silence I had never heard before. Such an emptiness. That is the moment I still remember vividly. A small point. A moment out of time, with everything ahead of me, and so few skills available to me. Before I had time to dwell on my inadequacies, the Principal returned with the key.

I opened the door and walked into my new home. It was a big two-bedroomed house, with two bathrooms and a kitchen. Unfortunately there wasn't much furniture. I had one bed with a bright pink mosquito net! One cushion chair, one desk and chair, and two buckets. These had been spread carefully around the house, to fill up the space. Three large ladies appeared with huge bowls of water balanced on their heads. In greeting, they all dropped on to one knee, spoke, rose again and went into the kitchen, giving me a shock but not spilling one drop of water.

106

The Principal had found the storekeeper, who looked like (and indeed was) a very powerful figure within the school. He had brought me a very bright light and something which I assumed was a kerosene stove. I hadn't seen either before, so he gave me an on-the-spot demonstration as he lit both. After this, the ladies, the storekeeper, and the Principal decided to leave me to it.

As they were leaving I said to the Principal, 'Please may I come to your office tomorrow morning to ask some questions about the school, and to collect my timetable?' The Principal froze momentarily before sliding into the car. 'I'd leave it until next week if I were you. Give yourself time to settle in. Goodnight.'

Had I known then that GTC Doko had only twenty-six students, or . . . or . . . many other things, I could easily have asked permission to leave, but optimism is a wonderful thing. I had arrived at my project, I had met the Principal, and if all went well I would soon collect my timetable and begin work. I locked the door and sat in the glorious solitude of my empty, echoing living room. No mud-hut life for me. What a lovely house. The heat from the stove reminded me that I should eat. I boiled water and ate corned beef out of a tin. Only now, five years later, can I occasionally eat corned beef without thinking of that night.

I decided that it was time to go to bed, as the mosquitoes were rather active. I had read the VSO handbook, of course, and was dressed as they suggested. In a long skirt, long socks, and a long-sleeved blouse I wasn't being bitten too badly, although I suspect I came dangerously close to heat stroke on several occasions.

Before I could go to bed to review the day's events, I had to solve three major problems. How did I switch off the stove and the light, and how could I use the bath etc.? After all, if there weren't any pipes to bring the water in, were there any pipes to take used water out? I managed to switch the kerosene stove off by disconnecting everything I could find, burning myself in the process. No doubt reassembling it would be difficult, but never mind.

The water situation was trickier. I didn't want to flood the house on my first night, but I did want to have a bath. After several experiments with cupfuls of water which disappeared satisfactorily I decided to bath, or rather wash, from the bucket. Inspired by the success of this, I finally plucked up courage to fill the cistern and flush the loo. Success! I collapsed exhausted on to the edge of the bath. What was I doing in a place where flushing the loo was a major triumph? I must be mad!

I was now more than ready to sleep. I locked up, and carried the tilley lamp into my bedroom. If you have never seen a tilley lamp, let me explain. It is a large, hot, blinding light with several knobs of different sizes to play with. I twiddled first one, then another, then another. I succeeded only in producing a sound not unlike a fierce rushing wind: I quickly switched that knob back to its original position and the light remained on. After several attempts to put out the light, I decided to leave it on. It used up my week's ration of free kerosene in one night, heating up my room to an amazing temperature and keeping me awake with its brightness.

In the early morning light, Doko looked clean and bright, but there still weren't any people about. There was a big brown dog outside the house, apparently friendly, so I didn't feel completely alone. The glistening fresh compound, and the blue, blue sky had my spirits soaring in seconds. To be able to sit on the doorstep in the early dawn, what bliss! I felt full of enthusiasm. Now at last I could go into school, collect my timetable, and find something useful to do.

My first few days in Nigeria had been blessed by good fortune. I wasn't ready for the problems which were about to face me. The Principal began to explain the school's organization. Firstly, I was the only teacher of English in the school. Immediately, any chance of working alongside someone and exchanging skills faded into the distance. I was on my own; was this going to help anybody? What was I doing here if I couldn't learn as well as teach? Secondly, the Ministry had 'shared out' some of our students as part of a reorganization campaign. On that day, the students of GTC Doko numbered twenty-six, all in one class. In order to give all members of staff some work, the timetable had included everyone. I was given two forty-minute periods a week, until further notice.

Two lessons, two forty-minute lessons. Was this what I had travelled over sand and sea for? How was I going to change the world in only two hours a week? What would I do with the other one hundred and sixty-six hours every week? How could I ever get to know Nigeria inside out if my contact with my students was so limited? Once again I wondered if I ought to throw in the towel and leave for England as soon as possible. But how could I go home? The Principal was such a nice man and all the other members of staff were so welcoming – not to mention that big brown dog. The Principal assured me that the new Form One boys would be sent soon, and no doubt other teachers of English would be posted to Doko before long.

After my initial panic, I thought for a few minutes and decided to get down to some lesson-planning. Never have I prepared so carefully. For my first two lessons I read through all my notes from the VSO English teachers' course as well as both the textbooks I had with me. I thought and scribbled for hours. Eventually I had what I thought was a perfect lesson or two. My visual aids were drawn, and then, finally, I was ready. Tomorrow I would begin.

The day dawned brightly, and I was up and dressed much too early. After wasting hours, I left the house at 7.25 a.m. in order to stroll gently into the classroom for a prompt start at 7.30 a.m. Inside the classroom I rearranged the desks, opened the windows, cleaned the board, and sat down to wait . . . and wait . . . and wait. At 8 a.m. I decided to go and find the students. How could they desert me in my hour of need? I walked round all the classrooms, but until I arrived at the Administration Block I didn't see anyone. Outside the Principal's office I found a messenger. By a mixture of languages, mime, and guesswork, I understood that I had chosen to begin my tropical teaching career on October 1st, Nigeria's Independence Day, celebrated as a national holiday. There wouldn't be any more lessons that week!

Being an emotional person at heart, I rushed away into my house and behaved as any other rational, mature adult would have done. I cried and cried – without the usual things to make me feel better, I luxuriated in self-pity. There was no chocolate, no beer, no people to talk to – what was I to do? I was a useless volunteer, unwanted and unneeded. I leave you to imagine the rantings and ravings of the next hour. If that big brown dog could talk, what a story he could tell!

Every volunteer that I have ever met has had low points where the question, 'What am I doing here?' is answered in a million different ways. Some volunteers give up and leave, many suffer in silence. In my case, I didn't have much time to think about it after October 1st.

Two days later two hundred boys arrived, many of them unable to read or write in English which they needed for all their subjects. We received a history teacher and a Nigerian Youth Service Corps PE teacher, and I became the English Department. All too soon I was teaching from 7.30 a.m. to 2 p.m. every day with remedial reading classes at night. There was the library to organize, a drama club to run, as well as the problem of boiling enough drinking water and eating sensible food. I didn't have time to think 'What am I doing here?' again until the end of that academic year, by which time my answer was much more coherent, although still very personal.

That was in 1978. It is now 1983, and although I have moved into secondary teacher training, I'm still in Northern Nigeria, still happy, and still, believe it or not, sometimes asking myself 'What am I doing here?'

13

PAUL HITCHMAN. Born 1953, Worcester. Worked as a herdsman and agricultural contractor before applying to VSO in 1978. He then worked as a volunteer agriculturalist in Sri Lanka, before moving on to become VSO's Assistant Field Officer in Zambia. He returned to the UK in 1982 and took a course in Estate Management at Seale Hayne College, Devon. He is currently VSO's Field Director in Uganda.

HAVING spent most of my early working life in agriculture, with the emphasis on the practical side, I felt myself to be leading a very insular existence. What was *really* happening in Britain and in other countries? Were the things I read in the papers always true? The questions seemed endless – and in many ways they still are. I had always enjoyed helping people, particularly those less fortunate than myself, for the simple reason that I got such a lot out of it. (I am quite sure that most of what we do, even the supposedly charitable, is basically selfish.)

One can soon become disillusioned working in farming in Britain, because of the relative isolation of most jobs, and the lack of any real opportunities for progress. Coming from a working/middle-class family, the chances of my getting my own farm were slim, to say the least. The thought of working hard and unprofitably for the next however many years in such an environment certainly did not appeal to me. I was determined to get involved in a more human and personal activity, like health work, for example. But what a waste of all those years of farming experience!

VSO had always been at the back of my mind; at school in Worcester, and then while studying for a diploma in agriculture at Seale Hayne College. However, it wasn't until a year after finishing college that I decided to send in my application.

Most people have heard of VSO; it's there in the back of our minds as something we might like to do, but most of us are put off for one reason or another. I hesitated to apply before finding out more about the people behind VSO. Who were the volunteers? VSO had always been viewed as a middle-class institution sending teachers to 'do their bit' in the ex-colonies. Unfortunately, this sort of image still lingers, and when I was interviewed and accepted during the spring of 1978, I found myself wondering what sort of organization I had become involved in. I was happy to find that other volunteers were just like me, with similar backgrounds, ideals, and motivations. They certainly weren't the group I had envisaged – over-religious, idealistic 'eggheads' out to save the world. It is a pity that VSO's middle-class image remains; it must make many potential volunteers think twice about applying.

I found I was posted to Sri Lanka. Most people who volunteer have little idea of what they are letting themselves in for. After spending most of your life in a European environment, a country like Sri Lanka comes as a bit of a shock – climatically, geographically, culturally, and economically.

Our arrival in Sri Lanka was, to say the least, subdued. We were completely dazed, and not at all receptive to our new surroundings. It was hardly surprising, considering the four-teen-hour flight, and the intense heat and humidity that greeted us. I shall always remember standing in the door of the plane before disembarking. As I went down the gangway I felt I was walking in to a very hot bathroom. My glasses steamed up and I gasped for breath. Was I really going to have to work in this?

We spent our first three weeks in Colombo, Sri Lanka's capital, getting acclimatized and continuing with our language training. At times this was very painful; but it wasn't until I arrived at my project that I realized just how important is a working knowledge of the local language. Many people in Colombo spoke English; however, in the rural areas the situation was very different. The management of a farm and the training of local counterparts makes some degree of fluency in the local language essential.

Anandapura Farm, my project, consisted of twelve acres of disused coconut-land which had been neglected for over twenty-five years. Since becoming overgrown, it had turned into a haven for illegal liquor distillers. I arrived near the end of the dry season, which had been particularly bad. As a result the farm, or what was left of it, did not look too good – 'farm' was really the wrong word to describe it: at this stage there was nothing there apart from a few vegetable and banana plots, and a beautiful bungalow. The livestock consisted of two rather emaciated cows, neither of which produced any milk, and both unlikely to be in calf. This didn't match the information I had received from VSO in London, and anyway, twelve acres is hardly a farm!

My welcome to Anandapura contained all the formality of Victorian hospitality, with ladies and children being packed off into the kitchen to prepare the food. Dr Bryan de Kretser, the project's founder, was there to settle me in and supply a little more information about my job. Anandapura was to be the second of two farms connected to Prithipura Infants' Home, which took in malnourished and physically and mentally handicapped babies. As the years went by and these babies grew, many would want the opportunity to live a more normal life, going to school, finding a job, and having a home. A farm seemed the sort of project to provide these opportunities, so the Prithipura Committee had invested in the Asokapura Farm, on a rubber-estate situated in the Sri Lankan hill country.

Asokapura proved a success, and had been running for seven years when Anandapura was founded. But where to start? As it happened, none of the people on the farm had any experience in agriculture, and we were not at that time in a position to discuss future plans in depth because my Sinhala was so limited. As the British Council van drove off down the drive I stood in front of the bungalow and looked – don't leave me! My new family (all ten of them) stood behind me, watching and wondering. I don't know who was the more worried, me or them! But during my twenty-eight months in Anandapura, these people were to become my second family, a family which captured my heart completely.

For the first month I ambled about making myself at home and viewing the land. The first thing to do was to find out what the local people felt they wanted, so I consulted Dr de Kretser and my counterparts. Their response: vegetables, cows, chickens, coconuts, etc. etc., whatever you would normally have on a farm: 'You're the farmer – you tell us.' All very well, but we deal with very different crops and agricultural systems in Britain. In the region of Sri Lanka where Anandapura was situated, we had a year which was basically divided into two rainy seasons (October to December and March to June) and two dry seasons (which covered the remaining months). This was excellent, because we had two growing seasons, which could be extended if irrigation was used, and it meant that agricultural development could take place very rapidly. After reading through many standard texts on tropical agriculture and consulting the local research and extension officers, I drew up a development plan which employed a simple farming system and yet was very intensive. In brief, I recommended that we should:

1 Remove old and unproductive palms.
2 Replant specific areas with new and more productive palms.
3 Establish a dairy herd of twelve cows to be zero-grazed in a purpose-built building.
4 Establish fodder crops grown under the coconut palms.
5 Establish 0.4 hectares of pineapple as a cash crop.
6 0.4 hectares each of vegetables and a pulse crop should be planted for sale and home consumption.
7 Establish a poultry enterprise of 400 laying hens housed in a deep-litter house.
8 Establish a small fish-breeding and growing project.

These recommendations were put to the Prithipura management committee and agreed upon, funds were allocated, and we were ready to move. However, it was unfortunate that at this stage I was admitted to the Gordon Frazer Nursing Home in Colombo with dengue fever. Apart from being a particularly nasty illness, it came at exactly the wrong time, with the rainy season about to begin and a lot of hard work ahead of us. All in all, the dengue fever cost me three weeks, a considerable setback in farming terms. Since my arrival at Anandapura we had cleared some of the boundary and arranged for electricity to be installed. All this was fine, but no crops had been planted and I wanted to take full advantage of the land we had cleared. It was all done by hand, apart from the final cultivation, during which we used a two-wheel tractor and rotavator – very hard work for three men in 35°C and 90 per cent humidity!

We agreed that cowpea would be a good crop – 'good food', I was told. So we set about planting cowpea. We had planted about half a hectare, a week of back-breaking work, and were pleased at the end to see the rain coming down gently. Disaster struck! That night, in November 1978, Sri Lanka's east coast was hit by a cyclone which devastated thousands of hectares of coconut and teak plantations, and made thousands of people homeless. Although the farm lay in the west of the country, we were severely affected. That night the heavens opened and the rain came pouring down, the like of which I have never seen before or since. The storm raged throughout the night. In the morning I walked the estate to view the damage – trees uprooted, tiles off the roof, and our plot of cowpea under six inches of water. When the water eventually subsided later that day we could see that much of the topsoil plus seed had been washed into our neighbour's paddy-field. What remained was rotting because of the waterlogging. This was a blow to everyone after so much hard work, but in contrast to the many Sri Lankan small farmers who had invested their savings in plots of land, we were lucky – at least we had enough money to compensate for the destruction.

Following the cyclone came drought, and a severe drought at that. We were able to ride the drought quite well, mainly because we had a good supply of ground water and only small areas of crops requiring irrigation. The coconuts and other tree crops fared well, since they had been well fertilized and mulched during the rainy season. This showed in the high yields of nuts from the farm throughout the year.

One of the major events of my first six months in Anandapura was the arrival of electricity. The nearest supply was located about a quarter of a mile away on the main road, so a line had to be erected between the power point and the farm. Because we were in a coconut plantation area, heavy machinery to erect the lines was out of the question. So, to overcome the problem of putting up the heavy reinforced concrete poles, we hired Mr Podisinga and his elephant (whose name eludes me at the moment, but in English meant 'Little Darling'). Having an elephant on the farm for a week does cause a few problems – for example, where do you put it? What do you feed it on? Each afternoon, after bathing in the nearby stream, the elephant was allowed to select a suitably tasty tree which she (with the help of her mahout) pushed over and carried to a suitable picnic place. By the time the elephant left for her next job, she had consumed a total of seven trees – the mess in the area where she slept and ate was considerable! But it was worth all those trees just to see the old man and his elephant work. Their relationship was perfect, and Mr Podisinga a master mahout. Although frequently drunk, he had little worry about how to get home. Often, after his day's work, he would sit drinking toddy in the bar until he fell over blind drunk. The elephant, sensing that he had had enough, would pick him up in her trunk and carry him home, as any true friend would. I was sorry to see them go, the little old man walking off down the road with his elephant trudging along behind.

At the beginning of the new year, our numbers expanded to twenty with the arrival of ten children from Prithipura, who were to make Anandapura their new home. In the coming months, the change in those children was quite marked. Better food and more attention, the chance to go to the local school, and the general environment of the farm had a real, visible impact on them. By the time I left for England in December 1980, the farm population had grown to include 25 people, 14

116

cattle, 400 chickens, 2 pigs, 4 dogs, 1 cat, 1 duck and thousands of fish.

The development of the farm continued apace during each rainy season. By June 1980 we had completed the cattle and poultry accommodation, the children's dormitory, and a second staff bungalow, and had started on an open workshop to be used by the more seriously disabled children. With most of the agricultural development on the farm completed, it was left to me to hand over the management of the project to Sirlpala and Diana, my two counterparts. This should have been straightforward, but the language problem came up again. All my notes and records were in English, and hence not readily comprehensible to my colleagues. To overcome this problem, each aspect of the project, along with the work required during each month, was transferred to a large chart and translated into Sinhala. So now, with the office wall covered with charts setting out the management of each part of the farm, my job was nearly over. My last project on the farm was in conjunction with Dr Mike Smith from Colombo University. This consisted of establishing a self-contained fish farm, a pet project of mine throughout my stay in Anandapura. The project involved digging a large trench in an undeveloped area of the farm. It was old paddy land bordered by a stream, and looked an ideal site for a fish tank. To do the digging we persuaded several of the expatriates working in Colombo to donate their labour for a couple of weekends. The digging project was a great success and provided high entertainment for the local population, who flocked to see what was going on. It was unfortunate, however, that I never saw the fruits of our labour, for after the introduction of the brood stock I left the country.

The leaving of Anandapura came upon me very quickly, and I didn't really know where my time had gone. My departure must go down as the saddest moment in my life. The Sinhalese on the farm had become my second family, and leaving them and the farm on which we had worked so hard, proved much more painful than leaving England. Perhaps it was because I felt I would never have the chance to go back, or perhaps just because we had been through so much together. I only know that on that Saturday night in December 1980 I broke down and cried like a baby when saying goodbye to the children and all the other staff. The next thing I remember was sitting in a crowded airport feeling very dejected and sorry for myself. Fourteen hours later I was in Heathrow and an English winter, dazed and sad, and yet fulfilled.

While in Sri Lanka I had decided to apply for an Assistant Field Officer's post with VSO. I wanted to work in another country in the developing world, which I could compare with Sri Lanka. VSO offered me a post in Zambia, and within two months of returning from Sri Lanka I was back at London Airport ready to start again.

14

PETER BRANNEY. Born 1957, Sale, Cheshire. Before VSO, he studied at Edinburgh university (BSc, Ecological Sciences). From 1979 to 1981 he worked as a volunteer forester with the Agriculture and Rural Development Department, Vila, Vanuatu. Peter re-applied to VSO in 1983 and is now working as a forester on the Community Forestry Development Project, Nepal.

TO THOSE who have never known it, 'culture shock' may have little meaning, perhaps summoning up visions of Victorian explorers expressing horror at the sight of naked men and women dancing around a camp-fire in the middle of a tropical jungle. At the very least it is a clichéd expression describing a vague feeling of disorientation on being put into new and unfamiliar surroundings. My own first impression on going to work in Vanuatu tended to confirm this view, and I laughed along with other expatriates over jokes about people 'going troppo' after spending too much time in the islands. In fact, it was not until some two and a half years later, during a short visit to New Zealand, that I actually experienced some form of 'culture shock', and as a result began to take the whole concept more seriously.

During my first few days back in Auckland from Vanuatu I seemed to be in the midst of a turmoil of fast cars, crowded tarmac streets, incessant TV and punk music, and all the time I felt these things were being thrust upon me from all sides. Perhaps it is unfortunate that readjustment to this sort of life is so rapid, and that after a few days so few of these fresh impressions remain. One thing which particularly struck me at the time, however, and which is still a vivid recollection today, was the sight of three New Zealand navvies, stripped to the waist and sweating, digging a hole by the side of the road with picks and shovels. In Vanuatu, to see any European doing this sort of physical work is a rare sight.

My work with the Forestry Department in Vanuatu was to help in the establishment and maintenance of small forest plantations scattered throughout the islands of the group. The ultimate goal of the project was to enable Vanuatu to become self-sufficient in medium-quality sawn timber, which was then almost entirely imported from Australia and New Zealand. The plantations are widely scattered throughout Vanuatu, for a number of reasons, the most important is the attempt to ensure that the benefits of the project in terms of cash employment during the early years, and the subsequent development of small-scale saw-milling and timber utilization industries, should not be concentrated in a single area or in a select group of areas. As a result, the project is active in the most isolated rural areas, those which generally are least likely to have any alternative forms of rural development at their disposal. At a local level, the plantations are managed by trained Forest Guards who supervize and plan the required forest operations, each Forest Guard being responsible for an island or group of islands.

Like so many Third World countries, Vanuatu is essentially rural, with more than 80 per cent of the population living outside the only two towns, Santo and Port Vila. To the casual visitor, however, this fact is not always apparent, or at least it can be easily forgotten. I particularly remember one New Zealander living in Santo who, although he'd been in Vanuatu for four or five years, suggested during a conversation that one of the main differences between Vanuatu and Papua New Guinea (which he claimed to know well) was that 'in PNG most people live in remote little villages in the bush'. What he thought 80 per cent of Vanuatu's population was living in was a mystery. It is in the towns, of course, where most influential people live, where most decisions are taken, where businesses prosper (and fail), and it is the towns which outsiders visiting the country tend to think of as being more or less typical of the country as a whole, simply because they spend most of their time there.

During my time in Vanuatu, the country's status changed from that of the Anglo-French condominium known then as the New Hebrides, to that of an independent republic. This transition was probably the most significant event in the country's history. The achievement of independence in 1980, coupled with the attempted secession by rebels in the town of Santo, catapulted the New Hebrides, as they were still called, into the international limelight. For a while, 'Stone-age tribesmen versus the Royal Marines' became a common newspaper headline. At the time of the rebellion, I was living and working on several of the outer islands where, contrary to the picture so dramatically painted by the world press, life was continuing much as usual, though we did hear a new and unusual topic of conversation. Later, I thought that this was the normal state of affairs: events passed by, aid projects came and went, offices were built, vehicles bought and plans formulated, all within one or both of the two towns. As far as development projects were concerned, the towns acted like a sponge, soaking up resources and releasing only a trickle to the people they were originally intended to help. Obviously, the problem varied from project to project. Even though the Forestry project on which I was working was one of the better projects in this respect, the uneven distribution of resources between rural and urban areas was still very apparent.

The small size of the country, combined with the nature of our project, had a very significant effect on my own position in Vanuatu. Comparatively few administrative levels exist between the Minister, who has overall responsibility for all agricultural and forestry matters, and the daily-paid labourer in the forest nursery. As a volunteer, my position lay half way between these two 'levels', and, in a sense, on the dividing line between expatriate staff and local people. This gave me a good picture of the social structure of the whole country, helped me see at first hand the operation of aid schemes and development agencies, as technical expert after expert passed through the country (usually in haste) on their various missions. Moreover, and perhaps more important, being in the centre of the 'ladder' meant that I could develop personal working and social relationships with people at most levels above and below me. One torrential afternoon in Santo was spent at the forest nursery experiencing at first hand the real difficulties of sieving soil and filling plastic planting pots under very damp conditions. Although there was shelter for the workers, the soil was too damp and sticky to be handled effectively. Later, I found myself dripping wet and muddy in a town office, shaking hands with the Minister and discussing recent forestry legislation.

Soon after my arrival on the project, the question arose as to what exactly was my role within the Forestry Department in general, and with the Local Supply Plantation project in particular. This is probably a question which arises sooner or later in the minds of most people working on development projects. In my case, there was certainly plenty of work to be done. Based in the town of Santo, at the centre of the communication and transport network for the northern part of the country, much of my time was spent touring plantations and visiting Forest Guards on outlying islands. When in town I helped to organize and arrange the collection and distribution of stores, planting stock, and information, to and from the islands. It was very easy to slip into a day-to-day routine trying to organize a hundred and two things at once, without ever really questioning the overall priorities – or my underlying motives. Perhaps working on a forestry project tended to increase this tendency, as I was well steeped in the idea that forestry is always a very long-term type of development. Within the space of two years (even when trees grow as quickly as they do in Vanuatu) there was going to be little prospect of getting a very clear indication of the success or failure of the project. The emphasis in forestry projects is on continuity, always with a view to the long-term effects of any action taken at the present. So, I saw myself, within the Forestry Department, as keeping a very viable project in motion, smoothing over day-to-day difficulties and stepping in to help out as and where needed.

The 'camp' on the forestry plantation on Pentecost island is about an hour's walk through coconut plantations and forest from the village of Loltong on the coast. As a result, when work is being done on the plantation, it is usual to sleep on site in the 'camp', returning to the village only at week-ends. Officially, I was supervising the work, mostly weeding and poisoning (removing the canopy trees which shade the lines of planted timber, using poison). Very quickly I found that supervising this work was extremely boring and frequently unnecessary, so it was not long before I took to wielding a bush-knife or hatchet and joining in the work myself. If I was later to be surprised to see New Zealanders digging holes, then the people of Loltong were similarly amazed to see me with a bush-knife, but they seemed genuinely pleased that my interest and involvement was of such a practical nature. Of course I was no match for the local people physically, as using a bush-knife is a technique they know from early childhood, but eventually the blisters on my hands hardened, the work seemed to become easier, and I became more or less part of a team. At the end of

122

each day, with every muscle tired and aching, I would join the group around the fire, talking and drinking kava, until at last, one by one, we would shuffle off to our bamboo bunks in a nearby hut.

It can be asked, quite reasonably, where the achievement lay in this? As a trained forester, ought I not to be using my so-called expertise to its fullest potential, rather than simply exerting myself physically with a team of daily-paid labourers? The answer is clear to me: my knowledge of the practicalities of supervising and actually doing the various jobs required on a forestry plantation was vastly increased by my direct experience. I could now approach Forestry Guards with confidence, discuss my supervision and its technicalities while actually understanding what we were both talking about, and I was able to build up a far better working (and incidentally, social) relationship with them. This kind of practical experience also proved invaluable later when I helped to compile a manual of forestry techniques for use by Forest Guards. The rate at which the different jobs could be done had until then been calculated on the basis of fairly haphazard guesswork; I could now lay down proper guidelines. Furthermore, the experience was of great personal value to me since it brought me into close contact with ordinary people who had ordinary goals and ideas. It certainly brought home to me the feeling that differences between them and myself were insignificant, and were more a result of different environmental and historical backgrounds than anything else.

Previously the Forest Guards had always acted on instructions from their bosses, who at the time were both expatriates. The bosses never did actual physical work, and the Forest Guards were given very little responsibility or room for initiative. My efforts were directed (admittedly unconsciously at the time) towards working alongside the Forest Guards proving in a practical way that the two sides were not necessarily incompatible. For a country which has suffered so much in the past at the hands of slavers, colonialists and exploiting Europeans, Vanuatu is, incredibly, almost free from racial tensions.

But the relationship between the European 'masta' and the Ni-Vanuatu 'boy' was still deeply entrenched, and I felt that whatever I could do at the personal level to erode this situation must have some effect on the independence of the country in its widest sense – people becoming aware that presumed differences of quality implied by recent history are not necessarily true or unquestionable. One aim, therefore, was to demonstrate to the Forest Guards that there was no essential difference in our respective capabilities.

From the point of view of a Ni-Vanuatu, it is hardly surprising that most visiting technical advisers and experts get things wrong. The visitors tend to spend a disproportionate amount of their time in the towns, rarely experiencing any actual involvement with rural communities. As a result, their personal relationships with ordinary, working people never develop sufficiently to overcome the built-in possibilities for misunderstanding. Fortunately for me, no one expects a volunteer to spend hours at an office desk compiling reports, or to make lightning visits to projects or entire countries. In fact, I was in an ideal situation to become genuinely involved with a community or with individuals while at the same time maintaining close contact with decision-makers. As a volunteer I had the time and the inclination to live and work with rural communities, something which (at least as far as forestry is concerned) no expatriate had ever really done before. This situation, which I feel is the key to the best use of a volunteer within a developing country, has two main outcomes. First, with regard to the actual project, its administration, and in many ways its success or failure, I felt I had an important part to play in the transfer of information, ideas and problems from the base of the pyramid to the top. Whether or not this really can be achieved in any given situation depends ultimately on how the volunteer is viewed by those at the top. Secondly, and to my mind the more important of the two, living and working among local counterparts can do much to build up confidence and responsibility on a personal level. In the long term it is only these qualities which will enable the goals of development,

124

whatever they may be, to be achieved.

Vanuatu is a small country and it is also a country with a fairly small population and with soil and climatic conditions ideal for the growth of food and other crops. Standing on a hilltop on the island of Santo, one of the larger land areas, looking down on the vast expanse of lush green and virtually undisturbed forest, it was clear to me that self-sufficiency, or perhaps more realistically, economic independence, were attainable goals. In my time in Vanuatu, I didn't initiate any vast new development projects or work any wonders with new plant varieties or seeds, nor did I find that my professional forestry training was of overwhelming importance to the particular project on which I was working. My presence there will soon be forgotten, but I think I can claim that I did demonstrate on a person-to-person level that economic independence need not be an idle dream nor need it require vast amounts of cash or expertise from overseas. Perhaps this sort of demonstration can help give people the confidence they need to work towards the goal of a better society. Only a drop in an ocean maybe, but perhaps the ripples will have a lasting effect.

As Julius Nyerere said, 'People cannot be developed, they can only develop themselves. For a while it is possible for an outsider to build a man's house, an outsider cannot give the man pride and self-confidence in himself as a human being'.

15

BETTY FORSHAW. Born 1919, Mussoorie, India. She spent a long career in librarianship before applying to VSO in 1979, including periods with the British Council in Delhi, the Nigerian College of Arts, Science and Technology, and the British Civil Service. Between 1979 and 1981, she worked as a volunteer in Funafuti, Tuvalu (South Pacific), setting up the National Library and Archives and training local librarians to take over her responsibilities. Betty's daughter, Penny, who wrote this chapter, served as a volunteer in Papua New Guinea.

I HAD been a volunteer in Papua New Guinea during 1973 and 1974, teaching a variety of subjects (English, Maths, Social Science and Agriculture) in a girls' boarding school run by a Roman Catholic mission. The experience had been enjoyable, exciting and invaluable, both as a practical way of showing concern for developing countries, and as an opportunity to share, however briefly, in the lives of those I taught. I was fortunate to be able to stay in the same villages, to sleep on the same floors, to wash in the same rivers, and to fight off the same mosquitoes as those around me.

I returned to England and trained as a social worker, but I kept up my interest in the work of VSO and joined the local Hertfordshire group. I gave talks to local societies and took part in fund-raising events like jumble sales, tombolas and barn dances. These events often involved my mother, who had been a keen correspondent during my years overseas and had regretted that the cost of a visit to Papua New Guinea had been prohibitive. At the age of fifty-nine, my mother had decided that the tiring travelling to her librarian's job in the civil service in London could not continue much longer. Sitting on half a *Financial Times* in the guard's van with a bowler-hatted fellow commuter had strengthened her view that rush-hour travel was not to be recommended! But she did not feel old enough to

126

stop working completely, and gradually the idea of working abroad as a volunteer took root. She applied to VSO and was accepted, and the wait for news of a posting began.

My mother retired triumphantly on her sixtieth birthday in April 1979, and took off on a fortnight's holiday to the Holy Land. VSO continued the search for a suitable project for an elderly librarian. Enthusiastically they seized on Tuvalu – formerly the Ellice Islands – and the establishment of a National Library based on the main island of Funafuti. Details of my mother's qualifications and experience were sent to the island and the delightful telegram returned: 'Forshaw posting confirmed, subject to physical agility'! My mother had visions of a fitness test in Belgrave Square, but the medical report allayed fears as to the state of this particular senior citizen's health.

The machinery of 'going out as a volunteer' began to move – descriptions of the project came in the post, and details of the various briefing courses she had to attend. The 'librarianship abroad' course began in London with half a dozen keen young volunteers in their twenties, and my mother. Their view of her was suspicious. Everyone seemed to know her: one of my friends who had been a volunteer with me in Papua New Guinea spoke of her library project, and one of their course lecturers turned out to know my mother from their work in the inter-allied book centre during the Second World War!

Very quickly, her departure date in September 1979 drew nearer, and soon the scene was Heathrow Airport – one volunteer to Tuvalu, two to Kiribati and three to Fiji, all on the same flight to Fiji via Auckland. My mother could scarcely carry her hand luggage, and suddenly remembered that she hadn't made a will. She disappeared through the departure gate, escorted by a charming Irish volunteer (who had already said his farewells in Belfast). Her last words were, 'Don't forget to let your brother and his wife have the silver teapot if anything happens to me,' and 'See you in 1981!'

Tuvalu consists of eight small atolls dotted against the immense background of the Pacific. My mother travelled around the islands setting up book collection points, but her main task was to establish the National Library, on Funafuti – an island with a population of around 2,000 people – and to collect together the National Archives. The archives were kept in a 'cold store' next to the Prime Minister's office in the Government Buildings.

Despite the absence of electricity and running water in her house, my mother appeared to adapt well. She learned to ride a bicycle again, on an airstrip, assisted by a warrant officer from the Royal Engineers (a team of whom were installing electricity for a part of Funafuti), and was soon describing the cycle ride from her house to the library: hens seemed to be the main hazard! From her photographs, the library seemed to consist of a prefabricated one-storey building with a corrugated iron roof. It did boast a sign saying Public Library, and the existing books were soon supplemented as orders went out and gifts came in. More shelving was added and unwary Pacific travellers found their paperbacks donated to the library from their yacht or ship. The *Benjamin Bowring*, part of the Trans-Globe expedition, called at Tuvalu and mother wrote of 'trading' some books, even with them!

Aspects of her life sounded idyllic, the lagoon and the warm sun for example, but there were also hazards such as grass allergies and travel on inter-island boats. My own experience as a volunteer in the Pacific made it easier to appreciate the illogicality and unreliability of local travel in Tuvalu. My mother often wrote of her companions on her travels. Phrases such as 'I shared a cabin with a nice young American man who was on his way to Fiji', could have been open to misinterpretation if one had not known that there would also be many other people sleeping on the floor of the cabin!

I was glad to read that she had found congenial companions among Tuvaluans and expatriates alike. There were several other VSOs and a New Zealand volunteer, who pumped my mother's water amicably in exchange for breakfast. She once remarked in a letter home that, 'I find my age doesn't stop me doing anything I want to do – but I can always use it as an excuse when I feel that I really want to opt out.'

Some aspects of librarianship in Tuvalu were to seep into VSO 'folklore'. While on a trip to the only secondary school, on the island of Vaitupu, the small boat in which she was travelling cut out over the reef and my mother had to half-swim, half-stagger ashore with books held aloft over her head. When this was featured in a cartoon in the VSO magazine, *Orbit*, I began to suspect a certain eccentric strain in the family.

During my mother's first year in Tuvalu I had returned to study for an MSc in Mental Health Social Work at Leeds University, and became sub-warden in a girls' hall of residence. The descriptions of life in Tuvalu continued to arrive at regular intervals. My mother's diet was spartan – it's difficult to grow vegetables and fruits on coral atolls as isolated as Funafuti, which had been hit by Hurricane Bibi in 1972 (an event commemorated in one of the many Tuvaluan dances). She made friends with the Tuvaluans who worked with her, and encouraged one of them, Kata, to pursue her librarianship studies in Fiji. When Kata returned to Tuvalu she worked alongside my mother and then took over from her as Chief Librarian when she left. My mother wrote that she had found the language too difficult to master, and that she felt that this was in some ways due to her age. This did not prevent her learning a few key phrases to keep the children in order when they came to use 'their' corner, complete with local mats and an attractive selection of readable books. The adult population were equally enthusiastic, especially over the westerns and the Mills and Boon romances the library had amassed, along with the wide variety of fiction and a good reference section on the Pacific itself.

Life as a volunteer in Tuvalu seemed rather different from my own experiences as a volunteer in Papua New Guinea. In some respects, this was because Funafuti was so small, which meant that everyone knew just about everyone else. It was quite likely that the librarian would be invited to official cocktail parties or dinner with the Prime Minister. These heady social heights were balanced by news that the 'fusi' (the small

129

co-operative shop) had no bread, no eggs and very few vegetables, but my mother had been thrilled to purchase a tin of
sardines! The lush quantities of fruit and vegetables so readily
available in Papua New Guinea, or even in nearby Fiji, were
not a part of the Tuvaluan scene.

One of the most valuable parts of my own experience in
Papua New Guinea had been the fact that my brother had
shared, at least, in the setting in which I had worked. He had
travelled to Papua New Guinea and journeyed home with me,
and I had promised to do the same for my mother. So, the two
years that she was away meant trying to build up a Pacific
Travel Fund.

I had been involved with VSO's Hertfordshire group as
secretary before I went to Leeds, and my mother had been the
group's sponsored volunteer. I had even helped with the spon-
sorship – 'Daughter pays for mother to go on VSO'. The local
paper featured this fairly accurately before she left, but succumbed to the greater sensationalism of 'Grandmother lived on
raw fish and coconut for two years,' when she returned! How
is the volunteer misquoted!

As September 1981 drew nearer our correspondence began
to reflect the impending journey – full of dogmatic suggestions
on my part and equally firm rebuttals on my mother's. We
were both agreed on visiting New Zealand, Australia, Papua
New Guinea and Nepal, but were at variance on other destina-
tions, the amount of money at our disposal, and the length of
time our journey would take. The local travel agents seemed
bemused at the mention of Funafuti, but eventually the plans
were finalized as far as Auckland, and I flew via Los Angeles to
Fiji.

After a night at the Suva YWCA and the prudent purchase of
pineapples at the local market, I headed for the airport at 6 a.m.
The Air Pacific flight only held six passengers; even worse, we
had to be weighed to ensure that the plane wasn't overloaded. I
was relieved to check in first! The three-hour flight began and
the neighbouring passenger asked my reason for travel: 'Oh,
you're Betty Forshaw's daughter! What a character! We'll all

be sad to see her go!' Sandwiches and coffee were served by the co-pilot in mid-flight, and soon we flew over a sprawl of atolls, the Funafuti group, shimmering sand and turquoise in the vast expanse of sea.

My mother had said that the island was small: this seemed an understatement as we came in to land. The airstrip seemed a short hop from oblivion. In front of the small concrete hut that served as the International Airport, the arrivals and departure lounge, and the customs hall, was a small figure jumping up and down excitedly – mother! I waved from the window while a policeman came into view and remonstrated with her. My fellow passengers let me off the plane first and we embraced warmly; mother then rushed behind passport control and customs – three feet of concrete counter-hop away – talking excitedly, telling anyone who would listen that I was her daughter. A friend took us in his 'moke' to her house and endless anecdotes and information exchanges began.

That night the local radio station proudly announced that Mrs Forshaw's daughter had arrived from England! My mother had just finished work and been given a farewell party by the Social Services Department, so we were able to use her last ten days to pack, explore, meet people, and bid them farewell. It was a joy to meet the friends my mother had made during the last two years – Kata, Mila, Sanwa, Tongiola, Rodney, Amanda, Martin, Jonathan, Neil – names which had often featured in her letters.

The library project had been a great success. It was a sizeable library in terms of books and a local girl had been trained as replacement for my mother. Mother's only regret was that it had not been possible to get a new library built – mainly due to the lack of a suitable architect. However, at a farewell party given by the Attorney General, the Public Works Department proudly unveiled a building block which bore the legend: 'Betty Forshaw, Librarian 1979–1981,' which they planned to install once they were erecting the building. I was overwhelmed by the high regard in which my mother was held by Tuvaluan and expatriate alike, and the necklaces presented at the airstrip when we left weighed us down. The term 'palangi lomatua' (old white lady) was used with affection and the expatriate population certainly seemed to view her as a local eccentric – perhaps it *had* been inadvisable to wear black plastic bin liners over a dress for arrival at the British High Commissioner's reception despite a thunderstorm – or to jump fully-clothed into the lagoon to cool off after work!

It is always hard to assess the impact a volunteer makes on their posting or the posting on the volunteer. My mother had always been adaptable, and welcoming, so I had not been worried about her ability to relate to new people or cultures. I thought her to be a competent librarian and her ability to organize the library in the two years she was there confirmed this. Our journey home gave me the unique opportunity to revisit my own posting seven years later.

I had said a rather tearful farewell to Papua New Guinea in December 1974. I still had friends among the nuns with whom I had taught, and we had arranged to visit them. First, though, we stayed with two Tuvaluan girls at college in Port Moresby, the capital of Papua New Guinea; they had been library assistants to my mother and had hoped to build up a collection of local legends from their islands. To see these gentle Polynesians hugging my mother and crying 'Betty! Betty!' was very moving.

I was delighted to find that girls I had once taught were now teachers in secondary, community and primary schools in their own right. Others were working in banks and hospitals. I had almost forgotten that warm affection – the hard hugging and clasping and shrieks of welcome – characteristic of Papua New Guinea. It was an amazing experience to walk unannounced into a local bank in Wewak and hear several of the cashiers shriek 'Eeh! Miss Penny' with genuine joy. We stayed at the school where I had taught, now with a predominantly Papua New Guinean staff and an ex-pupil of mine, Rita Kato, teaching English.

We eventually returned to England, to encounter winter, and society's misconceptions and incomprehensions of the outer and inner voyages we had made. My mother could be heard hissing, 'What civilization?' in answer to banal comments from those we met. The shops bedecked with Christmas frippery provided a stark contrast to the poverty we had seen and the material hardship in which we had shared, however briefly. Food and water are not commodities to be taken for granted – nor money, electricity, land or space.

You cannot live on a small island for two years without being affected by such an intensity of living, nor be able to sever those links with any ease. My mother found VSO's reorientation courses helpful, involving herself in her local VSO group and giving talks on Tuvalu. It took a year to resettle.

The Duke of Edinburgh summed up what we both felt to be our experiences: 'To volunteer for anything is to show concern, to offer to become involved. It is so easy to sit back and complain about the evils of the world, it is so simple to take the attitude that this isn't my problem. Protest and indifference have never changed anything; only practical involvement, conviction backed up by positive action has ever brought about improvement and better conditions.'

16

IAN RILEY. Born 1943, Liverpool. Before VSO, he worked in environmental management, becoming Assistant Director of the Environment for Swansea, and then Head of Landscape and Forestry for Buckinghamshire County Council. From 1980 to 1982, he worked as a volunteer civil engineer with the Bangladesh Rural Advancement Committee in Dacca. He then re-volunteered through the United Nations Volunteer Programme, and was posted to his current assignment as a Field Implementation Engineer with the UNCDF in Bhutan.

THE REQUEST for transport had not been welcome and the response arrived a day-and-a-half late. It appeared that a wireless message had been promptly typed but had then decorated a desk for three days, so instead of the new Toyota, a Land Rover appeared. A quick look was all that was needed to see that a day and a half was a short time in the aeons since it first left Solihull!

Our journey across Bhutan, to Timphu, consisted of two days of corkscrew bends. The first pass, Dochula, is low (at 10,300 feet) but spectacular: the tunnel of prayer flags, Buddha in his massive stone 'chorten', and then crystal air with nothing below for six thousand feet and a view up ten thousand feet to the snowy peaks flanking Tibet. Life should be full of such episodes!

An hour and a half later, with six thousand feet and five kilometres behind us, the bluest of blue rivers passes the spectacular Dzong, or fortress, at Wangdi. Wangdi houses the last petrol pump for a day and a half, to say nothing of a teashop swept by permanent forty-mile-an-hour winds. After Wangdi, the road, scratched out of the rock face, winds up to the next pass, Pele La, through wooded slopes and beautiful views, but with continuously dropping temperatures.

134

At 11,000 feet and above, the pass is covered with bamboo. People are entirely absent, but thousands of multicoloured, long-haired yak roam the slopes, probably the only animals strong enough to push through and digest the bamboo. At this point our driver must have been communing with his spirit when, after a clear road from Timphu, we spied a jeep approaching. It was the only vehicle we passed in three days, the road was straight (at least by Bhutanese standards), and we collided. Fortunately the laughter at such an inevitable happening caused more pain than the impact, and we continued on our way.

We should have treated the omens with more respect, for the spirits at all Bhutanese passes are powerful. At around fifty kilometres from the nearest town, with darkness and the temperature chasing each other down, and still at over 10,000 feet, I decided to call the vehicle to a halt. The trouble was simple: I was not happy at watching the rear wheel slowly overtake us. The last rays of light enhanced the beauty of the ice and snow, but hardly assisted in the diagnosis of our problem. However, it enabled the keen eyed to spot the white walls of a cottage near by, and the lone occupant stretched her meagre supply of food to provide a hot potato curry in time to prevent us stiffening completely in the sub-zero temperatures. Thermal underwear and a Mountain Equipment sleeping-bag helped me through, but the wash-basin, solid with ice though only three feet from the fire, encouraged speculation as to how a rug over the short skirt of the universally-worn male 'kho' prevented frostbite among our tender extremities. Was this the secret of Bhutan's low population growth?

The Land Rover looked a sad advertisement for British engineering at seven o'clock the next morning; repairing a differential with one spanner proved beyond our wit! We had the prospect of a fifty-kilometre walk to the nearest vehicle, but the thought that tourists pay 130 dollars a day to get a fleeting glimpse of the splendour through which we were travelling compensated for our increasingly wearied limbs. Six hours and about thirty kilometres later, the welcome sound of a road construction truck wafted down the track. How can you not like a country where nobody even questions why two odd foreigners, possibly the first our fellow travellers coming up behind had ever seen, should be marching down a road from nowhere to nowhere! Our previous day's destination suddenly appeared awfully close and welcome: but even at less than a kilometre away we still had more than an hour of bumping before our eventual arrival. This seemed an unimportant price to pay when our driver explained why he had used 'monkey gear' – neutral – as we coasted around bends above thousand-foot drops.

It's a strange feeling to enter a place which has dominated one's thoughts completely for two days, and find it beautiful but oh, so small. Weariness is a wonder drug for preventing worry, and the problem of where to stay solved itself when the district ruler, the Dzongdag, arrived and (comfort of comforts) carried us in his Toyota to warmth and whisky. Good food, eaten over good conversation, is hard to better in such a situation, and our gratitude was deepened by the Dzongdag's ordering another Toyota to be driven up through the night from the Indian border, so that we might be carried down the next day. Brilliant sunshine, a careful driver, more Japanese reliability, and a team of villagers called out at three in the morning to clear a rock fall from the road, saw us safely back. One thing we had to remember as we drove, this time upon a 'luxurious' surfaced road, through forest changing from alpine to sub-tropical, was that this was actually *work*; this was what good people in London (plus Geneva and New York in my case) had to sell as the 'hardships' of development. Hardships, of course, are relative; we were entering an area with tigers but saw only the footprints of golden lemurs (unique to Bhutan) and deer. Woburn was never like this.

Space signified our arrival at our destination on the Indian (Assamese) border; space created by the mountains simply ceasing. After thousands of kilometres through Tibet and Bhutan, the Himalayas stopped; we looked out over a vast void and then down to flat lands without end – images of two worlds. I had to remind myself that life was hard, and that hot water and a real bath were luxuries out of reach of most people in Bhutan.

Travel is only a means, and a $3 million irrigation scheme which had failed to start had been the reason for our journey. Next day we saw a group of Bhutanese Agriculture Department staff bowing to the inevitable and following two crazy Europeans wading up a river where Tarzan would have been at home. One gets to know one's national staff in their underpants! Two days, a lot of laughs and about fifty well-trodden kilometres later a scheme had evolved – low technology, relatively simple to implement and, best of all, merely following existing local practice. Optimism says it will work, but sadly it is almost inevitable that I shall be long gone before any real benefit accrues to the families living in the area. I hope lots of local staff will be, rightly, taking whatever credit is then going for the project's success, and I will be long forgotten. Maybe, too, a few more schemes could follow based on a thorough knowledge of local practice rather than on university textbooks. Maybe.

It was an uneventful journey, showing perhaps only that Bhutan is equally beautiful, whichever way you look at it, and that after too long in a Toyota one requires a retread to one's rump. A small price to pay.

17

IONA GORDON. Born 1950, Oxford. Before VSO, was employed as a community development worker and then as co-ordinator of Newport Women's Aid. In June 1983, she returned from Lusaka, Zambia, where she worked for three years as a volunteer Visual Aids/Publications Officer in the Communications Unit of the National Food and Nutrition Commission.

'IONA GORDON – I'm going to Zambia to work on preparing visual aids and publications for nutrition education at the National Food and Nutrition Commission.' 'Ah,' replied Dr Morley, 'so you've come across Fuglesang – a great project,' and he moved on to be introduced to the next volunteer who had come to hear the 'guru' of preventative health care on our VSO health-sector briefing.

Fuglesang? No, I'd never heard of him, so I rushed off to some appropriate bookshops to find out more. There I discovered books on *Applied Communication in Developing Countries*, *Communication with Illiterates* and other titles based mainly on Andreas Fuglesang's nutrition campaign in Zambia in the late 1960s. I began to wonder what work there was for me to do, when so much had already been achieved.

With great trepidation I arrived at my project, my brief being to set up a communications unit. My first surprise was that there were already three members of staff in the unit; a graphic designer, a photographer, and a radio producer. The second surprise was that these three had no idea who I was or why I'd come. I soon realized that the 'new' unit had simply changed its name from 'Public Relations' to 'Communications'. On discussing my position with the Executive Secretary, he gently explained that, while I wasn't establishing something new, it was hoped that I would breathe some life and inspiration into an existing, but dormant, section of the project.

The background to the project was as follows. Undernutrition is an immense problem in Zambia, as in most developing countries. It strikes hardest at young children. Here, out of every ten children born, four die before they are five years old. The Government felt that urgent steps had to be taken to find a solution to the high morbidity and mortality rates triggered off by poor feeding.

External aid flowed in to provide salaries for several experts, including Fuglesang, and to finance their research work. Results and numbers were the name of the game. A massive public relations campaign was launched, aimed at local communities, schools, field workers and government decision-makers. At the same time, a massive nutrition survey was carried out in seven of the nine provinces of Zambia. The irony was that the education campaign went ahead, with tens of thousands of leaflets, posters, radio programmes, textbooks and newspaper features, *before* the results of the nutrition survey were published. As a result, none of the promotional material (which is still available today) reflected the real problems of nutrition in Zambia.

The Zambian nutrition survey started in 1967 and finished in 1971. The survey was published, the campaign completed, and the experts moved away to other pastures. Without a doubt, the campaign was enormously successful in putting nutrition on the map. Wherever you go in Zambia you can hear mothers with underweight children complacently repeating their lessons. A rural woman who knows no English will be sure to know the words 'balanced diet' and 'hygiene', if only to satisfy her inquisitors that health education has been hammered home. The messages were clear – but how did they fit in with people's lives, and what practical effect did they have on improved nutrition?

Unfortunately, there is growing evidence to show that the nutritional status of the general population has declined over the last twelve years. This is closely linked with Zambia's declining economic position. In the face of such searing poverty

I began to wonder what nutrition education could really achieve. It is difficult to suggest to a pregnant mother that she should eat such and such to avoid anaemia when the necessary foods are not available, or are too expensive; or to ask her to look after herself and to make sure she has a reasonable share of the relish (any dish eaten with the staple maize porridge, or 'nshima') when traditionally she has only the pickings of what her man leaves behind.

The average Zambian diet is 80 per cent of the daily recommended calorie intake. Everyone is short of food. To improve this situation, what is required is better mobilization and redistribution of resources, by improving farming methods, food production, storage, marketing, transportation, basic health services, education and so on. However, to improve the nutritional status of infants, sick children and pregnant women, all of whom suffer most if there is a shortfall in food supply, there need be only a relatively small shift in the distribution of food that is already available to the household. Though the amounts involved are small, they make all the difference to the health of these vulnerable groups of people. It seemed to me that what was needed was a more realistic approach to nutrition, with solutions that could be carried out and explained in terms that mothers could understand from their own experience.

After making my own survey of education, by visiting rural and urban health centres and schools, I was even more convinced that our unit should make a greater contribution to supporting educators in their development work in different sectors. It seemed to me that there was very little health education material around, and what there was was old and out of date. When I joined the project, the morale and resources required to develop the communications programme were lacking. The unit had very high expectations of me because of the flair of the previous communications expert. Although I did not have the scope to produce materials on the same scale as he, this meant that I avoided creating such a dependence on a particular individual. Even so, coming from outside to a new country and new people, I found myself full of enthusiasm and ideas, compared with those who had been at the project for years. I found the pace excruciatingly slow at first. Week after week went by, and I thought, 'Well, what have I done?' finding little to show for my work. I had previously worked in two collectively-run projects and so tried through discussions to encourage a shared sense of responsibility; my colleagues would all too easily let me get on with the job alone if I appeared over-keen! Because, unlike them, I did not have a specific skill, I found at first that I had to prove myself and *do* things so that they would accept my presence. Usually, my suggestions were seen as veiled criticisms of their inactivity. This they sometimes admitted but blamed on the lack of finance to carry out work like printing. Once we had sorted out a plan of work, I found myself doing a lot of walking from one ministry to another, seeking co-operation and support over our plans.

After five months two of my colleagues left our unit, leaving the radio producer and myself. We immediately asked the management to take on a third member of staff to be my counterpart. He arrived eighteen months later! In the meantime, Mickie Mumba, the producer, and I persevered in the project; there was certainly plenty to keep us busy. Mickie expressed an interest in learning photography, and after a month's training his new skill enabled him to take charge of this side of the unit's work.

The demand for materials from different departments increased rapidly once the unit had gained a distinctive identity. The 'resurrection' was assisted by our early offer to help start a bi-monthly primary health care magazine called *Bwino*. I originally offered to do the pasting-up, but ended up (and still am) the Acting Editor, though we have been looking out for a replacement for some time. The magazine is published by the Ministry of Health and it was one of the proposals in the original primary health care document. Its aim was to be a link between the headquarters and the field by providing a forum for information, views, progress, suggestions and problems encountered in the implementation of primary health care (PHC). We decided to call it a health care magazine because we wanted to promote the fact that PHC is a concept of health care that everyone should be encouraged to support, rather than just a special branch of the health service.

Working on the magazine takes up about a quarter of my time. The other three-quarters are absorbed in the planning and preparation of various written and visual materials, editing reports for publication, assisting with administration, planning exhibitions (for example, for World Health Day) and agricultural shows, looking after visitors who come to collect materials, supervising the distribution of materials to schools, health centres, and farm training centres, and generally trying to make as much information as possible available to those who need it.

The actual output of the unit has been influenced by three main factors. Firstly, the implementation of the PHC programme in Zambia has led to the Ministry of Health, who do not have their own communications unit, looking to us for assistance in producing materials; their demand has been far in excess of what two semi-qualified workers can fulfil, but during my last few months in Zambia I shall be helping them to set up their own unit. This link with the Ministry of Health has oriented our unit's work far more towards the public sector than was the case originally. Recognizing that nutrition is intimately linked to other health issues, we have tried to show how lack of food, poor water and sanitation, poor hygiene, and preventable diseases all intertwine to debilitate and weaken people, especially mothers and children.

Secondly, the need for new ideas in nutrition to be promoted was long overdue. Accepted thinking in nutrition, as in many other development issues, has changed considerably over the last decade. In the past there has been too much emphasis on lack of protein in a diet, at the expense of a concern for energy-giving food. The basic problem is lack of food, not just of one type of food. Nutrition has been promoted by the 'three food groups' concept. This model of Protection, Energy, and

142

Protein is a simplified version of the western dietary pattern and does not coincide with the eating patterns of countries like Zambia. For example, it was taught that bread and nshima are both energy-giving foods. This is, of course, true, but to a Zambian there is no relation whatever between their staple nshima, without which one could not have a meal, and bread, which though very popular where available, is eaten purely as a snack. In addition, few foods have only one function. For example, groundnuts give both energy and protein, though they are classified as a protein food. With the help of the nutritionists we have been trying to develop materials which reflect recent thinking – stressing the need to increase the energy content of children's food, to feed children more frequently, and to increase variety in the diet from the selection of foods that are already available in the community.

The third factor that influences our work is the way education at every level is carried out. Education in Zambia, as in most countries, is very hierarchical. Creativity of thought is hampered by rigid adherence to exam syllabuses and non-formal education is also characterized by rote-learning. Discussions are rare, and non-literate students are often treated as though they hadn't a thought in their heads. I have been involved as a resource person in a series of seminars on communication skills and the use of visual aids in education. This is an extremely important area of work, and a new VSO volunteer has recently come out to help village workers in these vital skills of communication. Until informal education is approached through 'problem-solving' rather than rote-learning, and genuinely involves the groups at which it is targeted, community participation and self-reliance will remain unfulfilled.

The problems we face in the unit are daunting, and the longer I am here the more I realize how small is my own contribution. No doubt I could have produced more had I worked alone, but this would have been to defeat the object of my being here. Nothing should be static. Our materials are not permanent features – they must be adapted and new ones developed to fit in with changing needs. I am sure that in years to come others will criticize what we have done. But at least the PHC strategy is now discussed, considered, and analysed critically, at all levels.

One thing that pleased me greatly when I went home to South Wales on leave was that the women's aid group, of which I was a founder member and ex-co-ordinator, was flourishing, involving women of all backgrounds in mutual support and developing new initiatives in the community. My one hope is that in years to come I shall hear that the communications unit is providing a similarly useful service. With all the constraints in terms of equipment and funding, it does need a lot of determination and initiative to keep things moving. But with luck, my counterpart, Evans Mutanuka (who was appointed just before I started my third year), and Mickie Mumba will keep up the reputation the unit has now begun to gain.

We are hoping to acquire a lot of new equipment in early 1984 through an FAO-sponsored project. This is an instance where we have had to make a firm stand and say, 'We have manpower, we have no shortage of work, but we need the equipment to do it.' So many similar schemes end up by sending consultants to study the problems, who then come up with grand plans but are not around in the long term to implement them. With new equipment, the unit will be able to spend more time in the field developing and preparing materials with those for whom they are intended, rather than spending time as we do now going from place to place scrounging photographic paper, films, getting typesetting and headlines done, and so on. Despite the fact that we work all hours, the time we have to spend in scrounging and doing basic work has meant that we are only now producing the materials that were first proposed over eighteen months ago.

18

COLIN GREIG. Born 1955, Glasgow. Educated at the Glasgow College of Building and Printing. Before VSO, he worked as a Site Engineer for a number of different companies, and in 1981 was posted as a volunteer to the southern Sudan. Colin worked on the local Building Materials Extension Project in Juba, returning to Britain in August 1983. He has written two novels, as yet unpublished.

WHEN I joined VSO in 1981 my reasons were mixed. To be sure, I was worried about the current work situation in Britain, but I also had some thoughts about helping people. I have first-hand knowledge of bad housing conditions in my home city of Glasgow. That was why I went into the building industry, in the hope of playing my small part in eradicating sloppy workmanship. I worked on building sites for five years before joining VSO.

When I was first told of 'this project' in Southern Sudan, it did not fire my imagination in any particular way. I had dreamt of working on a tropical island, or in the mountains of Nepal. But I listened carefully to the voice over the telephone as he read out the job description. It was certainly a different kind of project, centred on the manufacture of one of the most useful building materials of all, bricks.

The project has now been under way for seven years. It was initially sponsored by Christian Aid, and technical assistance came from the Intermediate Technology Development Group (ITDG). At first the project was to introduce appropriate methods for the manufacture of local building materials, namely bricks and tiles. By the time I arrived on the scene, the sponsors were Euro-Action Accord, whose commitment to the project would end with me.

The aim of my project differed somewhat from that of the

145

previous advisers. They had set up the brickworks, while I was to extend the technology to outlying districts, establish a training programme, and introduce the latest appropriate methods. I took up the challenge and, after a brief course in alternative technology, I found myself full of simple ideas for improving this, that and the other. I also found myself in Juba, capital of Sudan's Southern Region. I'll never forget that first day. The only other time I'd left Britain was for a two-week holiday in Greece. It was hot there, but here in East Africa the heat was something else. Before I'd even reached the tarmac of the runway my clothes were soaked with sweat. The air seemed to be solid, and I felt I was drinking rather than breathing it. We were still in the rains and the humidity was 100 per cent.

I was never culture-shocked, though I admit to a racing pulse during my first few weeks of familiarization. During this period I succumbed to an ear infection caused by sweat. This, combined with where I had to sleep, led me to hate the place unreasonably. I tried to lose myself in the language course. I'm rotten at languages and this wasn't even classical Arabic: the version I was learning is understood only in the Southern Region. As luck would have it, most of my colleagues spoke a fair English, and they helped me to learn the basic Arabic of the town and the technical terms I needed for my work.

My dislike of the country vanished the moment the earache went and I moved into my house. Situated about four kilometres out of town, the house has no water or power supply and is at the end of a very badly pot-holed track. The scenery makes up for these disadvantages and now I'm used to bringing my water from town in oil-drums. I'm very happy here.

Problems soon began to appear when I picked up the threads of work left by the Canadian volunteer I had replaced. My work was to be different from his and it took some three months convincing the staff and workers of this. Even now I often find myself dragged into some day-to-day problem at one or other of the factories. I soon got into the Sudanese way of work, but found myself asking for help from the VSO field officer to try to specify the terms of my job a little more clearly.

146

Over a few days we managed to rearrange the job description into a more appropriate form, and finally I had my own line to follow.

I was often told that the previous 'khawaja' (white man) worked this way or that way, but it was not my way. I resented their unconscious references to my predecessor, and realized that the only way to overcome this was to prove myself in their eyes. My chance soon came. The Number 3 brickworks at Luri was nearing completion, but out on the floodplain there was no dry-season water supply. The Rural Water Development Corporation had been paid a large sum of money to bore a well. But the personality of my predecessor had clashed with the engineers and nothing had been achieved in eighteen months. My method was of calculated threat rather than angry remonstration. I simply reminded them by letter that they had had our cheque for one and a half years and had yet to drill the well. I added that if they did not begin before the end of the month we would take action to regain the money, plus eighteen months' bank interest. The following week the rig appeared and they brought in a well of sweet untainted water. I was one of the boys!

If it had taken time to settle in at work, I found that once I was in my own house I fell into an easy routine which gave me time to look around at my new environment.

As I mentioned earlier, the heat and the air were the first things to register with me. The air is incredibly moist, and full of the smell of flowers and vegetation. At certain times of the day it is also full of the smell of faeces! In a town like Juba, with no piped sanitation, few septic tanks, and a thousand or so pit-latrines, there is nothing for the rest of the population to do but to squat on the land around their 'tukuls' (thatched houses). The heat of the day sterilizes the excreta, but the dangers of disease and cholera are very real. When it rains, water supplies can easily become contaminated.

Food is an experience. Local delicacies are variations on commonly available European foods, but there are vegetables and spices and ways of cooking which make things taste very

147

different. Limited choice of food has made me eat things which I disliked in Britain. The suk (market) is amazing. Carcasses are pulverized by axes until the bones are splintered and smashed into the meat, which is cut up and sold by the kilo, bones and all. I seek out special cuts and pay over the top for them, but when cooking it's worth it. The market is full of noise, laughter and argument as people look for the best on display. Locals bring in their produce from surrounding villages and lay it out on sacking in 'kooms' (stacks) of equal quantity. You have to bargain for extras, or 'baksheesh' as they say here.

Other sights are more distressing – lepers sitting among the rubbish searching for a few morsels to eat; children with spindly, twisted legs, the result of polio, crawling in the dust kicked up by a passing car. These are sights that often make me angry, yet at other times I observe them with a strange cold impassivity. 'This is real,' I tell myself, 'this was once common in Britain.' It is something I can help prevent, in a tiny way, by making sure that brick technology gets to the outlying towns for people to build better houses for themselves.

There are about thirty VSOs in the Southern Region, and all became friends in the passing months. I'm surprised at the number of fellow Scots here, not just the volunteers but other expatriates in other aid organizations. Maybe it's a reflection on the state of things back home!

Once I had settled in at work, and all our workers had got used to me, I felt ready to begin the tasks I had set myself. Now I had never liked school, and all teachers were my enemies! I just could not see myself as a teacher of any sort, and so the training part of the project was delayed until I could devise a method in which I took only a small part. In the early days I placed greater emphasis upon new products and improving the quality of existing ones.

Our factories are labour-intensive. Of course we think we'd love to have big, beautiful, gleaming machines to do the hard work, but this *is* an underdeveloped country, and I have seen what happens to machines here: even simple diesel-powered donkey pumps have given up and fallen into irreparable decay;

the infrastructure is just not there. Roads are terrible, sometimes impassable, and fuel is needed in quantities which are simply not available. Mechanics have to be trained in every aspect of the machines' operation, and both tools and spares for repair work need to be available. With little money and poor communications sophisticated machinery is completely out of the question.

When ITDG came in, they looked for naturally abundant resources. They found them, appropriately enough, in the labour force. For the employees the work is reasonable, with wage rates similar to those of Government staff. The making of a brick is a long process. There is little that it is humanly possible to do here to speed up that process; little, that is, beyond the techniques we have already applied.

It might help to describe the way we make our bricks. Let's assume we already have a clay-field and an open pit, a large drying-shed (900 square metres), and a permanent roofed kiln. We have tools, wheelbarrows, and ample workers skilled in their own areas of work. We then dig some clay, digging deep so that different layers are mixed together. We make sure that it is free of stones and vegetable matter, like leaves and roots. The clay is then placed in a mixing pit for 'tempering'. This breaks down lumps so that the clay is ready for moulding.

We still use the ITDG hinge-mould, and one table can make up to 750 bricks in the course of a normal working day. This mould uses sand as the releasing agent rather than the water of the slop-mould. To make a brick, the mould is sanded, a clot of clay is rounded on a sandy surface and thrown into the mould. Excess clay is cut off and another clot is made. A pallet is then placed over the mould which is then inverted, the hinged base is raised and the brick slips on to the table. The new bricks are then carried to the flat surface of the drying shed. They remain there for five days, turned twice to equal the shrinkage through drying, and are then stacked for final drying. Depending on weather conditions, the whole process averages fourteen days. Add four days burning in the kiln and another four cooling, and the complete process takes twenty-two days. At best, we can make enough bricks for a kiln in sixteen days, so, weather permitting, the kiln is fired about every five weeks using fuelwood from areas allocated to us by the Ministry of Agriculture.

There are many stages in the process where things can go wrong and a little extra care improves the finished product. Bad mixing or excessive heat can cause cracking during the initial drying period. Bad handling of the fresh brick and an uneven drying surface are the main causes of misshapen products. Badly made moulds produce bricks of differing sizes. All these were problems we encountered during the first few months. I'm glad to say they are no longer problems, but to my mind this was just a part of why I was here. When another aid agency, ACCROSS (an international consortium of Christian development agencies), gave me the chance to do some field work, I seized the opportunity with both hands.

ACCROSS run numerous primary health care clinics deep in the bush. At the time they were planning to build a clinic in a village called Thiet, in Sudan's Lakes Province. They wanted to make their own bricks and asked me if I could help them. I would have preferred the initiative to have come from the Sudanese, but it was my first chance to extend my activities and I saw their work as important. So I found myself in a single-engined plane flying over the bush. There were some tremendous sights. We had to make three stops on the way, to bring supplies for other clinics, Thiet being three days away by Land Rover during the dry season. The landing strips were just areas of flat bush cleared of boulders and bushes. Every year they burn the grass, but problems do arise when a herd of cattle settles in the middle of the strip. Flying got worse as the day got hotter and thermals appeared.

Once in Thiet, I investigated two areas for clay-bearing soil. I was not encouraged, so went off to a third area, a waterhole. On the way the Land Rover was stopped by about forty painted tribesmen jabbing their spears at us and banging their shields. I thought my time was up. They were singing and laughing but were on their way to fight a nearby village for stealing some cattle. I was relieved when they disappeared and let us go on our way. The waterhole proved to be a place where Italian missionaries had made their bricks decades earlier. Half-ruined and overgrown, old school buildings could be seen as we walked through the undergrowth.

I had to stay in Thiet for two weeks until the plane returned on another milk-run. I'd brought a brick mould with me and so I made samples from all three areas. While they were drying I found and renovated a rusted Cinva-Ram. Then I taught three local lads how to use it to make blocks of reinforced earth, for building, and proceeded to make enough to build a small oven to fire the bricks.

The bricks from the water-hole proved to be good. Before I left I had time to teach the three lads how to make bricks using the mould, and I left it with them. I've had no contact since then but I did hear that the clinic is now fully operational. There were two lion attacks in the village while I was there. One killed a herdsman, the other killed a bull. I'd been sleeping on a verandah enclosed with mosquito mesh and chicken wire. I really wasn't convinced that it would stop an inquisitive lion!

Back in Juba I began experimenting. Successes were implemented, while failures were either forgotten or approached in a different way. The successes included the reintroduction of floor and roof tiles. Cost studies showed them to be far cheaper than either cement floors or zinc sheeting. Another success was the addition of sieved sawdust to the clay mix. This burnt during firing, helping to economize on fuelwood and producing a stronger brick. The most annoying failure has been in our efforts to make pipes. Small field drains are easy enough, but I'm trying to perfect a way of making 900-mm-long jointed pipes. First I designed an extruder based on the principle of a meat mincer. Wood would not take the stresses involved and metal is too expensive. So I'm back to a mould with a collapsible centre, to be tested over the next few months.

I made a clay-crusher, using an oil-drum to make the crushing heads. It needs some strengthening, but seems to do the job reasonably well. I think that the hinge-mould has reached its peak of performance in our factories. Certainly we can do no more to increase output unless we go on to the next logical step, and introduce the ITDG brick presses. I have ordered one from Kenya. When it arrives we shall make copies. But when training, we shall still use the hinge-mould method as it is easier to transport to outlying districts.

I started the training programme seven months ago, since when four groups have been put through the mill. It's not easy to get people interested enough actually to commit themselves to learning for a few weeks. I do not do any training as such, but merely organize it and bring the groups to the factory. Beyond that, the work is in the hands of the foreman, who is competent enough for both jobs. Each man is taught every aspect of brick manufacture. There are key points along the line, and when I visit the trainees I watch them closely, criticizing where necessary and giving praise where it is due. If successful, a trainee receives a certificate of competency.

One group has done particularly well. They come from a town called Mundri, about 150 miles from Juba, and were sponsored by their local parish youth group. They were eager and learned well. I gave them a brick and floor-tile mould free, and the latest I've heard is that they now have large drying and stacking sheds, and are making bricks. They have even requested roof-tile moulds, so they really have got into the swing of things. They are rebuilding their church first, and then plan to move on to houses for all the youth group. It is a small but positive step forward.

It is often said that the Sudanese are lazy. I find, however, that the people in the factories work hard *and* during times of stress. One woman I know, a water carrier, was nine months pregnant and worked right up to the day the child was born. She was given light work for the last month, and two weeks later was back at work. The child was sickly and had died. Many Sudanese walk miles through the bush to get to work. I saw one of our workers after he'd stumbled across an injured leopard. His leg was badly mauled, but luckily he's fine now. Another cheerful woman I knew had one leg grossly enlarged

152

with some disease. She held her job until she died suddenly. I've become impassive about death because it's such a commonplace thing here. But these examples do not support the stereotype of a lazy people.

I have dealings with a number of agencies, some of whom work closely on the refugee programme, to whom we supply brick moulds. They know the value of fired clay over mud and wattle; and they know that disease and ill health go hand in hand with unclean housing. With thousands of refugees in the area, an epidemic could easily wipe out both them and the locals. ITDG brickmaking technology is at least helping to reduce the dangers of disease by improving housing standards.

With six months to go, I feel I've achieved part of both tasks set for me. We can make special bricks on request, our bricks are the strongest in the region, and they do not dissolve in the rains. They are of uniform size and incorporate a 'frog' (the shallow recess in the surface of a brick), they save on cement, and are cheaper per cubic metre than local bricks. I designed a tiled roof which we've just built to advertise our products. I am pleased with that side of the work. As for personal training, I have a counterpart, though he is not, unfortunately, a particularly hard worker. Still, he may have learned something to his benefit. In any case, someone competent is always in control of the factories. The materials supervisor at the factory has the knowledge and ability to take decisions and stand by them. He is the hope for the future. I have a few groups still to come for training, and then it will be up to the supervisor and the engineer to make sure that others join the line. Outside aid ends with me. The brickworks will continue to produce, and I think quality will remain high. Time will tell.

19

REBECCA SCOTT. Born 1955, Newton Abbot, Devon. Trained as a nurse/midwife with Oxford and Avon Area Health Authorities (including a period as a paramedic in a Bangladeshi village hospital) before applying to VSO in 1981. She worked for two years as a volunteer health worker in Bangladesh before returning to the UK in 1983. She currently holds a temporary post as Health Development Officer with VSO in London.

THE FIRST question any Bangladeshi will ask you is 'Where is your country?' He or she will then ask the customary series of questions, the answers to which will enable him to build up in his mind a catalogue of all your living relatives, their occupations, marital status (your own, of course, having already been ascertained early on in the interrogation), and home. Fortunately, some get beyond these preliminary stages, and then, on hearing that we are volunteers on a salary comparable to their own, frequently ask 'Why do you do it?' I should point out that there are a great many Bangladeshis working outside their country, mainly in the Middle East, for financial reasons. Jobs commanding salaries sufficient for feeding, clothing, housing, and educating a family are few and far between in Bangladesh, and usually go to the relatives of those already in them. But this frequently-asked question has provoked me into thinking through my reasons for volunteering and now, with hindsight, the possible benefits of my work here. It soon became clear that these benefits were not as clearly definable as I had thought. But however intangible, however hard to assess, their ultimate value cannot be ignored.

To start with the obvious: why are volunteers wanted? The answer, in most cases, is to transfer practical skills to a counterpart. Any benefit to the volunteer – the opportunity to learn

154

about another culture, people, and language, and to learn how to use one's skills in different situations – is a bonus. As important is learning that nothing is as straightforward as it may seem, and that every problem has at least two sides and three possible solutions!

Then must come the benefit to the community in which the volunteer lives and works, and the community to which he or she returns. The former can never be quantified, but in a country where village television is becoming increasingly common, and thus 'the West' is viewed through the eyes of *Wonder Woman*, *Six Million Dollar Man* and *Dallas*, the importance of the alternative viewpoint given by the volunteer should not be underestimated.

Let me put these viewpoints into the context of my own experience. 'Gono Unnayan Prochesta's' (GUP) roots lie in a relief operation established just after the War of Independence in 1971. Despite steady emigration to India since Partition in 1947, there is still a high percentage of Hindus in south-west Bangladesh. They were hit very hard by the invading Pakistani army, who considered all Hindus to be guilty of harbouring pro-Indian sympathies and thus to be anti-Pakistan. Their houses were burned and their possessions looted, and those who escaped to India or who hid elsewhere returned afterwards to find their land had been occupied by local Muslims eager to take advantage of the situation. Thus the Rajoir area in Madaripur suffered, and still suffers, a great deal of poverty.

During the early 1970s Quaker Peace and Service Corps were allocated this area in which to work. They set up a number of centres for feeding severely malnourished children, as well as involving themselves in the distribution of seeds. The project was directed by foreigners, but involved several Bangladeshis from outside Rajoir as well as local personnel. When QPS felt that the time had come to leave, they were persuaded by senior local personnel to leave the buildings and infrastructure intact and to fund a development organization, to carry on the work they had started.

Since then (1973), the new organization, Gono Unnayan

Prochesta, has grown into a sizeable concern, now employing around 150 people. It is involved in all aspects of development and has programmes working with small farmers on co-operatives, with the landless on income-generating schemes, with farmers improving techniques and supplying seeds, with the illiterate in an adult education programme, and last, but not least, with the sick, in the medical programme. It is significant that although the correct name for this programme, 'Jono Shasta Sheba', translates as 'People's Health Service', it is always referred to as 'the medical programme'.

The medical programme started off very well, under the co-ordination of an excellent doctor who possessed the invaluable gift of being able to instil apparently limitless quantities of enthusiasm into his staff. He stayed for six years, in which time he built up a curative service of paramedics trained to recognize and treat common diseases (diarrhoeal diseases, worms, scabies, mild to moderate malnutrition, and chest infections), while referring other cases to the 'proper doctors'. This, however, was only part of their work; the rest of their time (four days a week) was spent in the villages giving help and advice, and teaching health education. One of the centres set up by the Quakers and run by two of the paramedics was kept open to treat children who needed more intensive care. Concentrating more on preventative care were eight Family Welfare Workers (FWW), whose prime objective was to motivate as many people as possible to accept family planning. This became an extremely successful programme, the key factors being that the FWWs put coils in the patients' homes, or in those of the FWW which by definition were close by, and that the workers were local people whom the villagers knew and trusted. After six years the project head left, and his place was taken by a doctor without a great deal of experience and, more importantly, without the charisma of his predecessor.

At this point in time all was not well within GUP. The new Director, enthusiastic and able though he was, was someone whose skills lay in public relations rather than in giving the whole project any sort of 'direction'. His reluctance to delegate

156

led to the suppression of initiative among senior staff. In his own work he treated GUP like 'one big family', a culturally appropriate idea in a country where so much importance is placed on the family, but impracticable when the family is as large as GUP. This paternalistic style of management has led to a very clumsy administration. Whenever the Director was away, owing to other commitments, very little happened. Another problem was that funding for the project was becoming increasingly difficult to find. In the early days of Independence funding agencies were less discriminating about the projects they helped, and the Director's not inconsiderable skills in public relations ensured a steady input of money. This allowed the project to expand, but provided no incentive for staff to establish income-generating schemes within GUP itself. Given the considerable land resources at their disposal, this should not have been difficult.

Now, however, foreign funds are more scarce, and donor agencies are looking more carefully at the recipient organizations and asking for evidence of effective utilization. GUP's programmes, though superficially good and based on sound principles, seldom stand up to this sort of scrutiny. The ability and motivation within the organization to produce the evidence required to guarantee funding is often lacking.

Within the medical programme itself curative work continued while the preventative work declined. This was because curative work tends to be more rewarding in the short term; without the inspiration of the programme's founder, long-term preventative care was allowed to lapse. It was at this point that I appeared on the scene, with the broad but imprecise brief of injecting new ideas into the programme. By working alongside the doctor, paramedics and Family Welfare Workers, I was to try to 'resuscitate' the project.

The previous year an outside team had evaluated the whole project, coming up with some good ideas about filling in the obvious gaps. However, they spent only three days in Rajoir and missed many of the important undercurrents in the project's make-up; hence the final report was probably more optimistic than the project merited. Nevertheless, their evaluation did provide me with important information, on the basis of which I was able to formulate an idea of what needed to be done and what I could do to help it happen.

In health education my ideas pointed in two directions: towards work in the villages, carried out by male paramedics using home-made flip-charts; and then towards the feeding centres, now known as the 'Children's Health Centre' or, again significantly, as the 'hospital'. The patients were admitted with their mothers and any other dependent children (usually those under three years old). The mothers were given an intensive course in how to feed the children and instructions in all aspects of family health and hygiene. The main problem was that there was no follow-up, so the teachers had no feedback on the effect of their teaching. There was thus no incentive to modify the teaching, or indeed to take much interest in it at all. Anyone who has ever been taught by an uninspired teacher will realize how pointless the exercise is. I was interested in using more exciting media for teaching, like puppet shows and plays. In an area where literacy is so low people don't really understand pictures, which makes flip-charts at best useless and at worst a distraction.

With the paramedics, I felt that they would be much more effective if they could include immunization in their village work. This required a certain amount of organization but was well within their capabilities.

As far as the FWW's were concerned, what worried me most was the absence of any sort of formal records. Apart from being an embarrassment whenever anyone asked for statistics, this meant that they had little idea of the effectiveness of their work. I also felt that the emphasis on family planning should be reduced and ante-natal care introduced into their work. In conjunction with these changes, I felt it important to train the village midwives in aseptic techniques, to avoid the many deaths of both mothers and new-born babies due to tetanus and other infections.

Having got this far, and been granted the necessary approval to proceed, it seemed a comparatively straightforward task to implement the proposals. This was not the case. It was, however, some time before I was able to pin down precisely where the problem lay. The obvious difficulties were really only symptoms of a deeper cause.

The answer came from the Director himself, one evening while we were sitting by a hurricane lamp discussing the problems we were facing in training the midwives. As soon as they had finished the course they expected GUP to employ them. The reasoning behind this was complex. Uppermost in their minds was their status in their community: they felt they had risked losing face by attending the course, tacitly admitting that they were not perfect. Another consideration was that this was a heaven-sent opportunity to supplement the family income. As I have mentioned, the family is of paramount importance in Bangladesh and it is often difficult to teach Bangladeshis to care for people outside their own family. Consequently, the argument that, by learning and practising what they learned, they were doing the community a service, cut little ice with most of our trainee nurses. The only argument that did make any impact was when we pointed out that their reputation was bound to increase if fewer of the babies they delivered died of tetanus. It was an impasse.

It was then that the Director, in his usual enthusiastic but roundabout way, explained that we'd have to go about it the long way round: organizations within the village had to start discussing health problems, and through these discussions would eventually come requests for training of their midwives. If this was what they asked for, they would presumably then take responsibility for them, pay them properly, and make sure they maintained proper standards. He was right; that was the only way to do it. But that could take years. On the other hand, doesn't any sort of major change in attitudes take years? As I listened to him, I suddenly realized that therein lay the crux of the matter. The paramedics were quite happy just doing their curative work, and the FWWs their family-planning work. They hadn't asked for a foreigner to come and tell them to do something else, and were thus not motivated to listen to what I had to say. I was asking them to change, and that was a painful process. In this way I learned that, unless a service is asked for, it is neither used nor appreciated. A lot of time was thus spent in motivating people to *want* training, time which might have been better spent in some form of practical activity.

Nevertheless, GUP now has an immunization programme, covering four villages and ten schools in the first year. I taught the FWWs the essentials of ante-natal care, and now one of them is herself capable of training in midwifery. The paramedics asked me to draw up a form they could use to assess the effect of teaching in the Community Health Centre when they went round on follow-up visits. I had had high hopes of the health education work. At one of the monthly paramedic meetings I had divided them into groups and asked each to prepare a short role-play on a different subject. They did so with great success. The other staff members, people from the building site near by, kids from the school, and people who just happened to be passing, all stopped to see what was going on, and stayed to laugh. Afterwards, however, nothing happened, until I heard one evening that one of the landless groups was doing a couple of plays in the village. Lo and behold, there before my very eyes I saw the story of Bablu, who ate sweets from Tekerhat and fell sick. He was taken to the 'fokir' (witch-doctor) and had magic water poured over him, was beaten with a stick and taken to the 'quack' doctor who gave him an injection of sterile water in an unsterile syringe. Finally, Bablu was taken to a GUP paramedic and fed a special rehydration mixture made from water, molasses, and salt (an idea of GUP's Director), which cured him, of course!

Thus, in my time in Bangladesh, I have taught counterparts and exchanged skills, both directly and indirectly. Nagen the paramedic can run an immunization programme, and Helen can run four ante-natal clinics a week in different villages, as well as teaching midwives how to prevent neo-natal tetanus. The villagers know it's worth it. They saw that, in the year before we started work, twelve children died of tetanus in one

160

village; the following year only one died, and her mother had refused to come to our clinic. The paramedics now go out to follow up their patients after they are discharged from the hospital, and the landless groups play out the story of Bablu.

During my stay I have learned an incredible amount about Bangladesh, the people, the language, and the culture. I have learned too, how to adapt my skills to different situations. Most of all, though, I have learned to be patient, and to appreciate that unless people are motivated to want something, it will be wasted. Vera Brittain, in her book *Testament of Youth*, puts it admirably: 'There is still, I think, not enough recognition by teachers of the fact that the desire to think – which is fundamentally a moral problem – must be induced before the power is developed. Most people, whether men or women, wish above all else to be comfortable, and thought is a pre-eminently uncomfortable process; it brings to the individual far more suffering than happiness in a semi-civilized world which still goes to war . . .' And she was writing after the First World War!

The benefit to the community in which I lived is not, as I said, quantifiable. I was the first westerner to stay for more than a few weeks in Rajoir, and so was the object of close scrutiny and much curiosity. As the people I lived with got to know me they learned that not all westerners are like Six Million Dollar Man or Wonder Woman. They learned that we don't all live in air-conditioned houses in Gulshan (the diplomatic ghetto in Dacca) and command vast salaries for driving around in Land Rovers. That can't be bad! I am sure that they have, if not a greater understanding, then at least a lesser misunderstanding, of the West.

Last, but not least, there is the potential benefit to the community to which I shall return in Britain. Intrinsic to the gap in wealth between North and South is a communication gap. Anyone who has travelled in the Indian sub-continent will know how hard it is to explain the realities of life here in terms people at home will understand. The sooner the gap is closed the better, and what better way to do it than by having westerners living, working, and learning in this sort of environment, so that they can educate their own communities, as well as having people from other countries working in England and learning about our way of life.

Victor Zorza has been writing a regular column in the *Guardian* newspaper about village life in India, and this week he has posed the same question as I have posed here: 'Why am I doing it?' His reply is slightly different from mine; he is primarily an observer whereas I am an observer secondarily, but I would like to quote a sentence from one of his articles that is as appropriate as any: 'It had gradually dawned on me that three-quarters of the world's people live in conditions of rural poverty that are not understood by the rest of us.' Not only seldom *known*, but, even when known, not *understood*, and that is, I am sure, a vital factor in the widening gulf between North and South.

20

JULIE BARTROP. Born 1955, Enfield, Middlesex. Educated at Bristol and Oxford universities, she worked as a scientific officer for the Scottish Marine Biological Association, and as a Biology Teacher for Stantonbury Campus in Milton Keynes. She applied to VSO in 1981 and was posted to St Theresa's Secondary School in Wamba, Kenya, where she is currently teaching chemistry and Biology.

FOR THE last eighteen months I have been a volunteer here at Wamba in a girls' boarding school in the arid bushlands of northern Kenya. The area itself is far less westernized than the rest of Kenya, and to a large extent, the local people retain the culture and traditions that are, sadly, fast disappearing in other parts of the country.

The local tribe around Wamba are the Samburu. Living and teaching among the Samburu has meant that I have been able to learn a great deal about a way of life which was at first completely strange to me. I have been fascinated by Samburu traditions and beliefs, and have tried hard to learn as much as possible about them: their reasoning, their emotions, and their way of life. To me, the most interesting of the Samburu's traditions is circumcision. It was certainly the most difficult to understand and accept. Circumcision was a word I seldom heard mentioned, let alone discussed, in England. In Wamba it is a word I hear almost daily in conversation both in and out of school. It is also a subject that appears frequently in the Kenyan newspapers, and is a major theme of much of East Africa's literature.

My first real introduction to circumcision and its important role in the life of the Samburu came when I attended the circumcision of a young local boy named Ndomonoki. Ndomonoki had befriended me when I first arrived in Wamba, and soon afterwards invited me to come to his circumcision ceremony, just as an English boy might invite you to his birthday party. He was aged about fifteen at the time and was still at the local primary school. I didn't realize quite what an honour this invitation was; it was only later that I realized what a huge step circumcision is in the life of a Samburu boy.

A circumcision can only take place when the moon is in a certain phase of its monthly cycle, so the date for Ndomonoki's circumcision had to be carefully chosen by the village elders. On the appointed day I rose while it was still dark, and set off through the bush to Ndomonoki's family homestead (or 'manyatta'). It was a beautiful morning, and the moon was still in the sky ahead, while behind me the sun was just rising over the mountains of the Matthews range. My feelings as I walked were confused – I felt apprehensive because I didn't know what to expect and I wasn't sure how I should react, but I felt excited at the prospect of being involved in what was clearly an important ceremony.

The sound of the warriors singing and chanting grew louder

as I approached the manyatta. When I reached the thorn enclosure surrounding the traditional hump-shaped Samburu huts, I could see a group of young men standing inside, some dressed in the red robes of warriors. I waited at the entrance to the enclosure until Ndomonoki's mother, Helen, noticed me and came across to greet me. She was wearing the special cloak of goat-skin reddened with ochre traditional among mothers of newly circumcised boys. As we walked over to her hut we passed the young men and I saw Ndomonoki and his two age-mates, who were to be circumcised with him, standing in the middle of the group. They were clothed in long black skins and clasped bunches of green herbs which Helen told me symbolized joy. Ndomonoki showed no sign of recognition when he saw me and he seemed to be shaking, almost as if he were in a trance. Helen told me they had been singing for over two hours, standing in the cold morning air, so that they would have become, by now, chilled to the bone. This, she said, would help to reduce the pain of the cutting.

The circumciser had not yet arrived, so I sat in Helen's hut with Ndomonoki's sleeping brothers and sisters lying round me on the skins. They were obviously oblivious to the importance of the day. The smoke from the wood fire stung my eyes and flies buzzed around my head. I was anxious for the ceremony to begin.

The atmosphere outside suddenly changed, and the rhythmic chanting of the warriors gave way to shouts and stamping. Peering out through the smoke I saw the old men, or 'wazee', running forward, their sticks held aloft in readiness for the traditional Samburu blessing. The circumciser had arrived at last, and as the group returned with him, I was surprised to see that the circumciser was my old friend Chakuya, the local blacksmith. I hadn't realized he was expert in circumcising young boys as well as making cow bells and spears – obviously a man of many talents. As Chakuya walked towards Helen's hut, Ndomonoki broke away from the group of young warriors and rushed towards us, his long black goat skin flailing behind him, his face contorted. His father and uncle ran forward and grabbed him, restraining him by his arms as he lurched forward uttering grunts and wailing snatches of songs. I couldn't recognize the young schoolboy I knew; I was frightened by the change in him and felt almost sick with fear at the thought of his ordeal. Helen sat calmly, looking on while I was wrestling to control my emotions, and she explained that Ndomonoki was not trying to run away, as I had thought. His father had told him he was to be circumcised after one of the other boys, and he was so desperate to be first that he had tried to fling himself on the ground in front of Chakuya in the hope that the decision would be reversed.

While my attention was focussed on Ndomonoki, Mori, the boy who had been chosen to be first, had been prepared, a crowd of onlookers gathering around his mother's hut. I left Helen and tentatively joined the fringe of the group. I was very aware of being the only person present who did not really know what was going to happen or understand what was going on, and Mori's circumcision proceeded, with me hovering at the back of the crowd, trying to pluck up the courage to move closer. While I was still deciding what to do Mori 'became a man', and the crowd suddenly surged across the enclosure towards Helen's hut, carrying me along with it. Ndomonoki's father called to me to move to the front and stand alongside his son. As I looked around from this favoured position, I realized I was the only woman present. Not even Ndomonoki's mother was allowed to watch this important moment in her son's life. She had to wait inside the hut to receive and tend to him after the ceremony. I felt I was being given privileges no Samburu woman could ever hope for.

A goat-skin was placed in front of the entrance to Helen's hut, and Ndomonoki leapt into view, completely naked, and jumped high in the air above the skin. He landed, his back to the hut entrance, his legs spread wide apart and his head bowed. As he fell, in a sitting position, a calabash of milky-looking liquid was thrown over him. I found out later that this was a mixture of milk and water which had been left out overnight so that it became as cold as possible: being doused with this mixture just before the cutting was another method of lessening the pain.

I could make out the figure of Ndomonoki's father, crouched in the gloom of the hut, one arm around his son's waist and the other resting on his bowed head. Two other men held the young boy's legs with the feet stretched wide apart, and I watched as the circumciser moved forward and squatted down between them, pulling a small knife from his belt as he did so. The first cut brought a stream of blood, and I felt sick. I stood completely still and watched with morbid fascination as Chakuya continued to stretch and pull skin, cut and remove flesh. Ndomonoki sat, his head bowed, milk dripping down his forehead, never even blinking or moving a muscle. Chakuya's hands were soon slippery with my young friend's blood, and still he had not finished. Discontented murmurs came from the assembled 'wazee' – this circumciser was not experienced; he did not know what he was doing; he was taking far too long; the pain should not be prolonged in this way. But still Ndomonoki did not flinch. I realized I was standing with every muscle of my body tense, my nails digging into the palms of my hands, my face contorted by imaginings of the pain my friend was suffering. I was astounded at the courage Ndomonoki was showing. I knew that Samburu boys and girls train themselves throughout their childhood to withstand pain in silence and with fortitude; now I understood one of the reasons why. Their favourite training method is to burn holes in their thighs using smouldering cloth; they sit without moving or displaying emotion while the holes burn deeper and deeper. Even small children of seven and eight years will do this. If a boy shows fear or pain during his circumcision he will bring disgrace upon his family's name, and will be beaten by his relatives as a coward. Even now, as Ndomonoki sat, the male members of his family were watching his ordeal with sticks in hand, ready to use them if he showed any sign of pain.

Suddenly Chakuya stood up and began cleaning his bloody knife. I heard Ndomonoki's father whisper to his son the words, 'You are a man'. The young boy's shaved head fell back against his father's shoulder and he began to wail a warriors' chant. He looked almost delirious and his eyes were glazed; but he was a man, a warrior now! He had come through his circumcision with bravery, and now he would be showered with gifts because he had honoured his family name.

I felt quite faint with relief that it was all over, and shaky through the effort it had required to stand quiet and motionless while watching what appeared to me a mutilation of a young friend. The actual cutting had taken over five minutes, but an experienced circumciser can perform the operation in only two or three minutes. To me it seemed more like an hour.

Confusion broke around me as most of the men moved away to the next hut, where Matenye, the third boy, was waiting for his initiation into warriorhood. Ndomonoki's close family stayed with him. His uncle slipped the special goatskin shoes, made for a newly-circumcised warrior by his mother, on to his nephew's feet. The first time his feet touched the ground as a man he must be wearing these shoes. His father and several other 'wazee' then gently lifted him up and moved him to his mother's hut. In the gloom and smoke inside he would be placed on the special raised bed of sticks and matting his mother had prepared for his recovery. I was still standing outside in a sort of daze when I heard Ndomonoki call me. Quickly recovering myself, I turned and entered the hut. It was so dark inside that I had to stand still in the doorway before I could see anything. After a few moments I made out the shape of Ndomonoki, crouched on the bed in the corner, his head resting on one bent knee. He looked very dejected and I could hear him making the odd clicking sounds the Samburu make when they are in pain. I moved over and sat down beside him. I felt completely inadequate to help him, but I felt a rush of emotion as I told him how brave he was and how proud I was of him. The younger children had awoken and were staring at their brother; Helen sat by the fire on a goatskin calmly watching her son. All was quiet except for the low moans and clicks from Ndomonoki. I heard a shout outside and realized that the third young boy, Matenye, had attained warriorhood.

167

There was a noise at the door and two old mamas came in to congratulate Helen on her son's courage. They sat down with her by the fire, and one of them reached over and pulled a goat's stomach from behind where I was sitting. Samburu store their food in the strangest places! Helen began chopping, handing out pieces of raw stomach lining for us to chew on. I had tried this before, but, feeling sick, I decided not to join in. I declined politely, saying I wanted to go out to congratulate Ndomonoki's father, but I would come back. I stumbled out of the hut, thankful to get away from the smoke and smell for a while, and found Ndomonoki's father grinning from ear to ear with pride, discussing the fee for the ceremony with Chakuya. As I greeted them I was called by three young warriors to go and help in the bleeding of a cow, for the first food the newly circumcised boys would eat was to be a mixture of fresh blood and milk. I went over to the animal and watched as they tied a rope around its neck to restrict the blood vessels. After a minute or two, the blood vessels began to swell. One of the warriors then knelt down and fired a wooden arrow at point blank range into the animal's neck, but his shot was unsuccessful, as was his second shot. The third, however, produced an arc of blood from the animal's throat. This was quickly caught in a calabash. The poor cow strained against the rope and closed her eyes as I stroked her nose. They let her bleed for some minutes and then suddenly, without warning, she broke away and careered, bellowing, across the enclosure, with blood still spurting from her neck. I tried desperately to get out of the way, but I couldn't decide which way to go. My indecision nearly resulted in my being barged into the thorn bushes, but luckily the young warriors caught the cow by the tail just before it reached me.

I waited until another cow had been milked and then I helped to mix the warm blood and milk together in a calabash. I took it over to Ndomonoki in his hut, where he told me he hated blood and milk, surprising in that it was one of the favourite foods of all Samburu (or so I thought). His mother told him he had to drink it, so he took the calabash and drank from it while I sat on the floor with Helen, and watched her finish cooking the goat stomach. The warriors usually eat the rest of the meat and the intestines are always saved for the womenfolk, who stew them and apparently find them very tasty. Suddenly Ndomonoki lurched forward from his bed and vomited on the floor. The ordeal, followed by blood and milk, had just been too much for him. He lay back and moved around trying to find a position in which the pain wasn't so intense. He was still naked and I could see his wound surrounded by swollen flesh and congealed blood. He was covered in flies, but no-one made any attempt to clean him up or help to make him comfortable.

Helen gave me the calabash of blood and milk and told me to drink as it was very good. I peered at it and decided it looked a little like strawberry yoghurt, so I took a deep breath and drank; it was a pity it didn't taste like strawberry yoghurt too! At that point Mori's mother came in to congratulate Helen on the bravery of her son. Quickly, I took the opportunity to offer her a drink and relieved myself of the calabash. She was very happy as Mori too had shown only courage during his circumcision.

I was beginning to feel very tired, and decided that it was about time for me to head back to school. I looked at my watch and was surprised to find it was only 7.30 a.m. Although I had left my house at 5 a.m., I felt as if I had been up for much longer. I explained to Ndomonoki and his family that I had to go back to school to teach, but that I would come back later in the day to eat and celebrate with them. I was worried about leaving Ndomonoki as I was sure that his condition would worsen during the day. I couldn't see how his wound would not become infected with so much dirt and so many flies around. When I returned, I would bring my antibiotic powder. Ndomonoki's father escorted me to the gate, and promising to come back after school, I hurried away through the bush, hoping I would not be late for Form Two Chemistry.

I was only a few minutes late for my lesson, but appeared in the laboratory looking rather tired and dishevelled, and so I told the students where I had been and they were very surprised – it seemed they did not expect their Chemistry teacher to be interested in such things. They were also happy that I was beginning to learn something of the life their boarders left when they came to school, and to which they returned during the holidays.

Most of the girls I teach are circumcised, as are all their brothers of warrior age. They were so eager to tell me more about their traditions that my planned practical on acids and alkalis was discarded, and we spent that lesson discussing their views and feelings on circumcision. They were able to explain a lot of what I had seen and had not fully understood at the time; I think they were pleased and proud to be able to teach their teacher for a change. The more I learned, the more I realized how difficult the transition must be for these girls when they return to school from home each term. From living in a mud hut with no facilities, wearing skins or pieces of cloth, and spending their days collecting wood and water, and herding goats and cattle, they return to life in a brick building with electricity and running water, western-style beds and a school uniform, and lessons from morning to night. I was glad to hear that they enjoyed both life-styles and most could see good and bad points in each. It would be sad if coming to school led these girls to lose interest in the traditions of their tribe and to despise their families' way of life.

That evening I returned to Ndomonoki's manyatta, armed with my antibiotic powder. To my amazement, I found him much better, up and walking around, though with his legs rather straddled. Just two days later he proudly arrived at my house attired in the long black skin of a newly circumcised warrior, carrying his bow and arrow. For the next few weeks he would spend his time shooting birds, which he would then use to decorate his headband. His words as he left that day were, 'There is no problem now; I am a warrior and I fear nothing.'

Circumcision is just one aspect of traditional Samburu life, and the day I have described was one day in the life of one volunteer. The story does illustrate the conflicts which can arise when one is confronted by a culture which is alien and challenging; but that I shared in Ndomonoki's circumcision was an immensely enriching experience for me.

21

PETER HALSTEAD. Born 1953, Solihull, West Midlands. Before VSO, he worked as a House Physician at Basingstoke and St Alban's hospitals, and on the G.P. Vocational Training Project for Northamptonshire Area Health Authority. He also spent a year teaching in Zambia between 1971 and 1972. He is currently working as a volunteer Medical Officer in Kandrian Health Centre, West New Britain Province, Papua New Guinea.

KANDRIAN is the main government 'outstation' on the south coast of West New Britain, one of the provinces of Papua New Guinea. I eventually arrived here about six months after the previous VSO doctor had left, largely owing to the long delay while I waited for my visa application to be approved. My job was to succeed him as District Medical Officer for the Kandrian District, described as being 'responsible to the Provincial Health Officer for the proper provision of health services to the Kandrian District'. This proved to be a brief which belies the simplicity of its description; the job is much more wide-ranging than I had ever expected. During my time in Papua New Guinea I have learnt that the practical problems facing 'poor' countries cannot be solved as easily as I once thought. There is so much that needs to be done here in improving and developing health care that the one year I have left is unlikely even to allow me to scratch the surface of the problem.

171

The village of Kandrian itself has about 400 inhabitants, almost all of whom are employed by the government in a variety of institutions: Kandrian houses the district offices of the government, responsible for the administration of a huge but sparsely populated district with about 150 miles of coastline, extending inland as far as the central mountains. The whole district contains only around 17,000 people, and with such a scattered population communication is a major problem, canoes or feet still being the main modes of transport. In addition to the local administrative offices, Kandrian also boasts a High School, a Vocational (Technical) School, a prison, a bank, two stores and a health centre, the main one for the district. Fortunately, there are only four other expatriates here, the local priest and three teachers, one of whom is also a VSO volunteer. Unlike some places, there are not enough to form a clique. Consequently, relations with the local community are always good, with no hint of anti-white antagonism. In fact the opposite is true, with local people holding us in a position of unwarranted and sometimes embarrassing respect.

Although this small community is isolated – the only transport in or out being either a boat or light aircraft – its isolation has helped to preserve its beauty. To describe it as 'idyllic' would be a cliché, but in this case appropriate; how else can you describe an area of coral reefs and small off-shore islands, each one having white sandy beaches lined with swaying coconut palms. It's the type of place I had previously associated only with 'Martini' or 'Bounty' advertisements, and yet the scenery is a necessary part of life because its very presence provides an escape from the pressures which inevitably develop in any small community, particularly if you happen to be the only doctor.

The health centre is the focal point for all health activities within the Kandrian District. As such, it also functions as my base, although my responsibilities encompass the whole district, with several smaller health sub-centres and aid posts. The scope of my duties is equally broad, stretching beyond the

172

clinical role for which I have been trained, to administrative, supervisory, and even political or diplomatic roles which I have had to learn by trial and error, and which have proved far more taxing than the familiar clinical work. There are forty in-patient beds at the health centre which are frequently full, with additional patients having to sleep on the floor or outside in the kitchen, or even under trees, a situation we should view with horror in Britain but which is accepted quite readily here. There is also a busy out-patient department which sees 50 to 60 patients a day, so there are times when I find that I'm in danger of becoming tied to Kandrian because of the workload here, and I have to keep reminding myself that I'm also responsible for the rest of the district. I see a wide variety of conditions from the strictly tropical, like malaria, leprosy and parasitic infections, to familiar conditions of western medicine, such as chronic bronchitis, pneumonia, gastro-enteritis, and tuberculosis, which declined in Britain as living standards rose but which are still prevalent in Papua New Guinea. I can perform minor surgical procedures in our small operating theatre, but as I have only basic surgical training, I try to refer all major surgery to the main provincial hospital. Unfortunately this depends on their being an appropriate flight at the right time, and on a few occasions we been forced to proceed here in Kandrian. At these times the scenes are reminiscent of MASH, with the surgeon reading the surgical textbook before he starts, the operating assistant being only partially sighted as his glasses had broken on the previous day, and cans of corned beef being stacked up outside the operating theatre as 'rewards' for the blood donors! Fortunately, such emergencies are rare.

The staff at the health centre are willing workers, providing they are shown clearly what to do, but the easy-going Melanesian nature does not readily adapt to change. The result is that new procedures, or changes in treatments or methods, may be accepted initially, but unless there is constant checking they are soon overlooked or forgotten, although not deliberately ignored. Similarly, routines, without which no hospital can function, are very slowly accepted, and changes of routine are even more difficult to implement. The problems do not end there. Both our nurses, Jean and Augustina, are married with children, so it is not unusual for one of them to be absent because one of the kids, or the baby-minder, is sick. And of the four hospital orderlies, Aiom is illiterate, Tembe can read large capital letters, and Andrew and Pulpulio both wear glasses – in fact they share a pair, the same pair that was broken on the day before the emergency operation! These are not meant as criticisms of the people of Papua New Guinea; they merely illustrate the realities which make improvements in health care difficult to achieve. We do, of course, apply constantly for more trained staff to be sent to Kandrian, but there is a regularly negative response. In a country as young as Papua New Guinea, there simply are not enough trained staff available. In any case, as in most countries, qualified people tend to stay in the comfortable surroundings of the towns, rather than return to rural areas.

Despite these difficulties, working directly with patients gives obvious and immediate rewards. To see an emaciated, weak, coughing child transformed into an active, plump bundle of mischief after two months' treatment for tuberculosis, or a bedridden, depressed, wheezing bronchitic become a cheerful old character about the town with the use of simple medicines to improve his breathing, are the things that keep me going. But the reality is that these individual successes are insignificant when compared to the mass of illness that we never reach. Only a small proportion of the population have access to ante- and post-natal facilities, provided by nurses at four small health sub-centres throughout the district, while the remainder of the population are served only by aid posts. These are manned by orderlies with a bare minimum of training to enable them to deal with malaria, simple infections, and cuts and grazes, and there is usually one aid post to every six or eight villages. But even then there are some places where the nearest aid post may be four hours' walk away. Four hours' walk in this humidity is tough enough for a healthy doctor, but it must be just about impossible if you also happen to be anaemic, undernourished, and suffering from malaria. Clearly many people are receiving far from adequate health care, and if overall standards of health are to improve, it is in these areas that we should be concentrating our efforts with preventative and educational programmes as well as curative medicine.

This is the other main aspect of my work: to develop health services within rural areas throughout the Kandrian district, and it is this side of the job which I have found most difficult. Firstly, it is difficult even to find time for this part of the job, because the pressing needs of patients at the health centre always seem more immediate than the more nebulous task of health planning and organization. Secondly, even if plans are drawn up, there is no guarantee of their being carried through, since the Papua New Guinea bureaucracy is notoriously slow and inefficient, and money is so scarce; the recession in the West has hit the economies of the poorer countries even harder.

Rural health care in Papua New Guinea is based on a hier-archical system of provincial hospitals, district health centres, smaller health sub-centres, and village aid posts. The doctors work in the hospitals and larger health centres, while the various other institutions are run by people with progressively less training, thereby ensuring that resources are well distrib-uted in terms of skills, and the maximum coverage is achieved in terms of areas served. In practice, however, the system does not work as effectively as it might. There are not enough primary health workers to provide adequate coverage, and those there are do not always work as effectively as they could. Many are old and find it difficult to adapt to new treatments and methods, especially if they are unable to read. Others are younger, but are unwilling to accept the responsibility that accompanies the job. Although health patrols, health educa-tion, and basic hygiene are part of every primary health worker's job, they are all too easily overlooked when super-vision is lacking. The easy answer is to train more health workers, but training costs money and, for the time being at least, we have to make do with what we have.

The reality of working in Kandrian is that these problems have to be resolved as effectively as possible under severe constraints. Thinking about the wider issues of health and health care, I realize that two years is really not long enough even to start large new programmes, let alone see them carried through. Nevertheless, one has to try. I try to get out of Kandrian as much as I can to visit the bush aid posts and also travel along the coast to the other health sub-centres in the district. If nothing else, at least this shows that someone is interested in their work, and I hope it elicits some sort of response in terms of meeting the needs of their own particular areas. Such visits also provide me with an opportunity to assess local problems and try to remedy them through the various official committees and channels when I return to Kandrian. I plan to organize a week's training course in Kandrian for the staff of the district, but so far these plans have been thwarted because of staff shortages and transport difficulties – either the hospital vehicle has been out of action, or else the roads have been flooded. However, even in Kandrian one can pressure the various government committees to redirect resources to the areas of greatest need. This diplomatic role is completely new to me, and I still lack the polished technique of the local public servants and politicians. Results can be obtained far more quickly with the aid of support from local politicians – we may even have our new ward by the end of the year, despite the financial cut-backs, with a little 'greasing', as it is called in the local pidgin.

Diplomacy also comes to the fore in handling staff and personnel problems, another new field for me, but all part of the job. What to do about the orderly and his family when their house and belongings have all been destroyed by fire? How to settle the differences between two married staff members when the wife is brought to the health centre following an aspirin overdose? And the commonest problem of all, how to arbitrate between members of staff and their creditors, a situation which frequently ends with me as banker acting for the creditor, and deducting instalments from the wage packets at source. It can

176

never be said that VSO projects lack variety.

There is, of course, more to being a volunteer than just the project itself, and there is more to life in Kandrian than medicine. Half the enjoyment of being in a developing country lies in seeing, and being a part of, a totally different culture. Of course, one can never be fully accepted, and there are aspects of Papua New Guinea life that I would not wish to accept anyway. But equally, I have learnt much from Papua New Guinea culture: the importance of the family in looking after the sick or elderly, the ready acceptance that there are not cures for all diseases, and attitudes towards death, with none of the fear and undignified clamouring for life which typifies western societies. I have also found a people who are able to enjoy life to the full, despite lacking the material benefits so important to people in the West. The village 'sing-sings', in which the whole village takes part in traditional singing and dancing, are still common events, often for no very good reason (but then why do you need a reason to enjoy yourself?).

Perhaps I could end with the story of the Christmas pig? After discussing the matter at a health centre staff meeting, we decided that it would be a good idea to buy a pig for Christmas, and cook it in a traditional 'mu-mu' for the staff, their families, and the patients. We planned to buy some local fresh fish, and then ask the local villages to donate sweet potatoes, vegetables, pineapples, pawpaws and other fruits, to make a more than adequate feast. The staff agreed to donate K5 each (1 Kina = 80 pence), and I asked the local businessmen and government officers for donations before they went on their Christmas leave. We ended up with K100, of which I designated K60 for the pig, K20 for the fish, and K20 for drinks. The fish was bought at the market, the drinks were bought at the store, and with a week to go I had three offers of pigs which had to be assessed. Not knowing much about pigs, I asked our driver to see them, so with five days to go he went to see the first one, and returned saying that the piglet he had been offered certainly was not worth K60 and would scarcely feed half the required number of people, so the following day he set out again. This time he found that the asking price for the second pig had gone up to K80, and the third pig was no longer on the market as his owner had decided not to sell. Undeterred, he told me his brother had two smaller pigs which together would be more than adequate, and he only wanted K50 for the pair, so with three days left he went to see his brother and returned empty-handed – his brother would not sell. With two days to go we still had no pig and I could see all our plans falling flat, but then the health centre cook came to our rescue. He offered us his pig which he valued at K90, saying he would pay the missing K30. Gratefully I negotiated with him, and as I parted with K60 I wondered who was coming off the better, but eventually, on Christmas Eve, we had our pig. It was cut up in the afternoon, ready to be cooked overnight, but when I visited the health centre in the evening all was far from quiet. Our 'butcher', who was also one of our hospital orderlies, had stolen all the entrails, including liver, kidneys, heart, the lot. These were essential to a good mu-mu – when the meat is wrapped in banana leaves and slowly cooked by being covered with hot stones – so I was sent off to recover them, much to the disgust of the 'butcher' who regarded them as his rightful fee. Eventually the pig was cooked, with the cook sleeping next to his culinary creation overnight to ensure that there were no further attempts at theft. On Christmas Day we all gathered together, staff and patients, and enjoyed a very filling meal, and I must confess to a smug satisfaction when I heard one of the patients say, 'Dr Peter's a good doctor, he got us a pig for Christmas!' So much for clinical acumen!

22

LINDA MANNING. Born 1955, Haverfordwest, Dyfed. Before VSO, she worked as a staff nurse at St Bartholomew's Hospital, London, and as a staff midwife at Bristol Maternity Hospital. She is currently working as a volunteer Nursing Sister with maternal and child health teams at Kwapalim, Menyamya District, Papua New Guinea.

I ARRIVED in Papua New Guinea in October 1981 to work as a nurse/midwife with the Lutheran Church in the Menyamya District of Morobe Province. Menyamya is divided into two sub-districts, Menyamya and Aseki, with a total population of 40,000. I came to live and work in Kwaplalim (in the sub-district of Menyamya), looking after a small health sub-centre, with three aid post orderlies (APOs) and running a maternal and child health team with three nurse aides.

Kwaplalim lies at 1,400 metres above sea level in a small valley surrounded by beautiful mountains covered in 'kunai' (sword grass), merging into the bush as one goes further from the settlement. At Kwaplalim we have a small community school serviced by six teachers (all from other areas of Morobe), a health sub-centre (with the staff mentioned above), and a couple of trade stores. Kwaplalim shares most of the characteristics of similar-sized settlements throughout Papua New Guinea.

Ikumdi, one of the areas in which we worked (or 'patrolled'), lies approximately twelve hours' walk from Kwaplalim, in the Gulf Province of Papua New Guinea. In January 1982 Dan, a local pastor and a native of Gulf Province, was sent out with his family to work in Ikumdi. Since his posting Dan had always made a point of asking the volunteer sister based in Menyamya to work in establishing clinics in the area. At that time she and her three nurse aides were the only maternal and child health team serving the entire population of 40,000, whereas in other provinces each such team served between 4,000 and 5,000. Understandably, she felt unable to undertake a major expansion in her work.

With my arrival, together with the District's second maternal and child health team, we felt able to visit Ikumdi. After talking with Dan, we arranged to go and hired a small number of men to help with our cargo. As it was a hard twelve hours' walk, we decided it would be easier on the carriers (not to mention ourselves) to break the walk into two days. Dan assured us there was a small garden house (a house erected for me while the villagers prepared and worked their gardens) in which we could stay at the end of the first day.

So on a fine Wednesday morning in September we finally started our patrol to Ikumdi. It was 7.30 a.m. and our patrol consisted of Dan and five carriers from Ikumdi, myself, five nurse aides (two borrowed from the Menyamya-based team), one aid post orderly, the work 'meri', who runs the church work and women's courses, and our three dogs – Jose, Cleo, and Blackie.

Walking, the only way to travel in many parts of Papua New Guinea, has many rewards. The people you meet and the scenery you see more than compensate for the effort involved; once a walk has been completed you tend to bask in a smug feeling of satisfaction as you reflect upon the journey.

After a few hours of walking we reached the bush, which offered us more protection from the sun and heat. But the bush also brought with it a large mountain, one of four we had to climb to reach Ikumdi. After three hours' walking we took our first break at a lovely ice-cold mountain stream, resting for about ten minutes, drinking the cold water and eating pineapple. Unfortunately one of the nurses, Mete, had malaria, so was not feeling at her best and had already vomited, but after our rest she felt slightly better and wanted to continue.

The next two hours' walking were pure hard slog – up and up, until finally we reached the top of the mountain, assuming

180

that by now our garden house *must* be fairly close. As often happens on reaching the top of a mountain, the cloud and mist had fallen so we were unable to see anything. Never mind, we rested, talked and joked among ourselves, and questioned Dan and the Ikumdi carriers about how far we still had to go before reaching the garden house. This was a stupid question to ask any Papua New Guinean, especially a Menyamyan, whose 'klostu tasol' (close to, that's all!) can mean anything from ten minutes' to three days' walk! Nevertheless, we were all reassured that the house was very close.

We left the top of the mountain at about 1 p.m.; three hours later there was still no sign of the house, and we were struggling through deep bush, thicker and damper than before, and bringing with it a greater variety of wildlife. Jose, one of our dogs, killed an opossum, much to the delight of the carriers, who managed to take it off him before he devoured it. Leeches were also in great abundance, delighting in this unusual surplus of food. Still we walked on, climbing yet again, but all the time fooled by 'klostu, klostu'.

By 4 p.m., after eight-and-a-half hours' walking, and still with no sign of the promised house, we started to pressure Dan. Now he told us that we could make it to Ikumdi in a day – in his eagerness to get us to come he had invented the garden house as an inducement. So we plodded on, having no choice since we were in the middle of the bush with no shelter available. The carriers were beginning to feel the strain (as were all of us) and one young carrier started to cry. One of the stronger, older women took the youngster's cargo as well as her own.

At 6 p.m. we were still walking, with no sign of Ikumdi; it was getting darker and cooler and then began to rain. As we got more and more tired, showers became more frequent and tempers shorter. Just for one fleeting moment, I thought it might all be a hoax and we were being led into a trap.

It became increasingly obvious that we wouldn't make it to Ikumdi, but still we walked for another hour and a half until 7.30 p.m., when we found a makeshift shelter. The bush

181

wasn't so dense here, and in the clearing stood a small dilapidated house; no house had ever looked so warm and welcoming. However, we later found that the two boys who were carrying our kaikai (food) cargo had gone on to Ikumdi as it it was only about one hour's walk away – so, no food!

All fifteen of us huddled under a leaking roof, around a fire and Coleman lantern. The carriers proceeded to skin the opossum – the intestines were given to Jose to eat, but we quickly devoured the meat. Some of the Ikumdi came and gave us sugarcane and water, so we sat for a while before getting down to sleep. While unwrapping my sleeping bag, I found the most enormous leech I'd ever seen. This was quickly disposed of and I made a thorough search of my bag before putting my head down.

I awoke at about 5.30 the next morning, slightly stiff but surprisingly refreshed. Gradually we all surfaced, breakfasted on some taro (the staple diet of this area) and quickly packed up. We set off for Ikumdi with none of us willing to believe how close they kept telling us it was. But this time they didn't lie – after crossing a river and one last small slope (made difficult by the slippery mud), we had our first glimpse of Ikumdi, through a clearing in the bush. The inhabitants had actually moved to this area only the April before, so all the houses – made of wood and pandanus leaves – were new and only some were completed. The new village had been built near the top of a mountain on a stretch of land free from bush, the idea being that they could build an airstrip near by.

A group of boys had run on ahead to tell the people of our arrival, calling others by blowing on a large conch shell. It looked beautiful, this lovely new hamlet, surrounded by a wooden fence, with the people of Ikumdi gathering to greet us. Just one more small hill to climb before we were welcomed by smiling faces and firm handshakes, and a magnificent view of the four huge bush-covered mountains over which we had walked. This was my most emotional moment since coming to Papua New Guinea. The rest of Thursday was spent washing, drinking, eating, and story-telling with the people of the village. They were amazed that we'd even bothered to walk out to see them.

The villagers were far healthier than the Menyamyans we'd left behind, basically owing to their better diet. Being located in the bush, the village had a plentiful supply of vegetables and meat – birds, rats, opossums, and frogs. The big river which we'd crossed also provided food in the form of fish, freshwater crabs, and prawns. I began to wonder whether it wouldn't be better for us to leave them alone!

That night Dan held Lotu (a church service) out in the open, with bush light to sing and read by. We were all introduced again, and announced that we should be holding 'bebi skel' (a clinic) the following day. Friday dawned another lovely morning and James and Leban, two Ikumdis, made a makeshift table for us; we used Dan's house to hang our health posters on. As with most of our clinics, we were to hold it outside. We had attracted the whole of the village. First of all I told them what our job was, emphasizing the preventative aspect of health care and playing down our curative role.

Unfortunately, Papua New Guineans, just like everyone else, prefer to concentrate on curative rather than preventative health care. Health workers tend to perpetuate this preference since it involves less effort on their part. In Papua New Guinea the main curative method is of 'suts' (injections), usually of penicillin, which are seen as a panacea for all ills. People request or expect injections for every ailment, with the result that many have developed a resistance to penicillin, due to over-prescription and incompleted courses. We hoped to be able to counteract such thinking through our work in villages like Ikumdi.

We weighed the children (very frightening to a child who has never seen a weighing-machine) and then began the difficult task of estimating their ages and birthdates. Since Dan had started working in Ikumdi, we had given him a calendar and record book in the hope that this would encourage the villagers to tell him when they had given birth. Before becoming an evangelist Dan had had some experience in basic health care, so some of the groundwork had already been done. But I felt that the villagers were doing many things – like washing regularly, and building toilets – simply because Dan told them to, and not because they accepted these things as improvements in themselves. But with luck that would come later. I had seen the effects of lack of washing in Menyamya, where badly infected scabies is almost endemic.

As we saw each family and examined the children, we talked with them (through an interpreter) about some preventative health-care measures. Generally, people in Papua New Guinea don't start feeding their children on solids until their teeth begin to appear. In a normal healthy baby, this is at about 5–6 months, but in Menyamya people, especially women, are malnourished. In consequence, babies are born malnourished, given an inadequate milk supply, and they stay malnourished. Growth is slowed down so that teeth appear at as late as 8–10 months, resulting in even slower growth rates because solid foods are not given until teeth begin to appear. It is a vicious circle. Here in Ikumdi this wasn't such a problem because people were generally better nourished. But on talking with them I discovered that they believed that to give a child with no teeth solid food would prevent his or her teeth from growing at all! This was a reminder to us health workers of how the cultures and customs of a 'developing' country can affect health and health care and must always be considered when attempting to provide health services and education.

The final aspect of our health programme in Ikumdi concerned vaccinations for the village children and basic ante-natal care for the women. Here, vaccinations start at the age of two months, not six months as in the UK. Our ante-natal care programme consisted of taking histories and weighing all the pregnant women. I found this was a more caring society than the Menyamyans: here a woman would go out to deliver in the bush with the help of another woman, whereas the Menyamyans would go out on their own, unaccompanied and unaided.

We examined the women in a small cookhouse, with the help

of our carriers to interpret for us. This was difficult because they spoke two different languages: they could understand each other's language, but couldn't speak it. We showed the women how to massage their wombs in order to cut down the blood loss in case they began to lose too much after delivering.

That evening was spent sitting around story-telling; in Papua New Guinea this is a way of life. We were using Dan's house and his pit toilet. His toilet was a bit too sparsely covered for our liking, as you could be clearly seen using it during daylight: consequently, there was a mad rush for the loo as soon as darkness fell.

The next day was to be 'nutrition day'. The villagers killed a pig for us and prepared a great 'mumu' (cooking food in the ground on hot stones). We gave demonstrations of all the different food groups and their value, stressing that it was important to eat some food from each group every day. Surprisingly, they didn't know how to cook food in bamboo, so we demonstrated this, using the food the people had brought – bush ferns, pumpkin, etc. When the demonstration was over, everyone enjoyed tasting the results.

We were to leave the next day (Sunday), but our aid post orderly, Malachi, was to stay with the village for two months, practising preventative health care, touring the area (Ikumdi was made up of three separate villages), and advising on improvements in water supply and sanitation.

Now, five months later, I think our visit was successful. The villagers were interested and keen to learn, and were never afraid to ask questions. But as always it was I who benefited most from the experience, teaching simple health care in a uniquely different setting. We plan to visit Ikumdi again at the end of February, if the rains don't prevent us by making the river unfordable. We walked home from Ikumdi that day by a different, longer route – but that's another story in itself!

23

JILL AND HENRY NEUSINGER. Jill was born in Alex-andria, in 1929. She worked as an actress with the Bristol Old Vic and other companies, and then left the theatre to go into farming with her husband. Henry ('Turf') was born in London in 1928. Before taking up farming he also worked on the stage, including a period as stage manager for the Library Theatre in Manchester. In 1981 Jill and Henry applied to VSO and were posted to the Redd Barna Rural Development Project at Udawelayagama, Habarana, Sri Lanka. They are working on experimental dry-zone farming techniques.

IF YOU climb the 500 feet to the Rock Fortress of Sigiriya, as we did to mark our first Christmas here, you get a superb view and a good feeling for the shape and make-up of 'the Dry Zone' of Sri Lanka, which covers about one third of the country and the whole of its northern area.

This is where King Kassepa, after murdering his father and usurping the throne, built his remarkable palace fortress and entrenched himself for thirty years, during the fifth century AD. From Sigiriya he saw, as we did, the jagged skyline leading up to Kandy and the hill country twenty-five miles away to the south, the Minniyera reservoir, or tank as it is called here, glinting in a gap in a low line of hills twenty miles to the east, and to the west and north, a jungle-covered plain broken only by a few rocky outcrops like the site of the Sigiriya fortress. As the king searched the landscape for his avenging brother, he would have seen many of the same tanks, large and small, which are still visible today, for they were part of an irrigation system built by an even earlier king. In December they would have been gleaming full of water; in July and August, dry and smooth and interspersed with columns of smoke and bare burnt patches, where the chenas (clearings) were prepared under the ancient system of shifting cultivation. Still further to the north of the Dry Zone lie the white asbestos roofs of the village of Udawelayagama, almost hidden by the jungle. This was our home for two years.

Turf and I arrived in Colombo, Sri Lanka's capital, in October 1981. During our two-week language course we were introduced to Redd Barna, the Norwegian 'Save the Children' organization for which we were to work. It was a short acclimatization, and I remember feeling fairly bemused as well as impressed by the confidence of some of the volunteers we met, who had already completed over half their service here. How would *we* be feeling in fifteen months' time?

Redd Barna have nineteen projects in Sri Lanka, mostly in community resettlement and agricultural development, in both Sinhalese and Tamil areas, and also in Colombo. Their staff are all Sri Lankan except for the Resident Representative (then John Westborg) and his deputy. We met them both, together with Stan Burkey who was to take over as Resident Representative in May 1982, to talk about our project. The idea was to try out some alternative ways of developing a small resettlement holding, within the context and financial limitations of the village and unhampered by the constraints of professional competition felt by the Sri Lankan staff. 'Yours is an innovatory role,' John said. 'Just try things out and keep ideas coming. Failures are also successes.'

He sent us away to think about it for six weeks, telling us to travel the country as much as we needed, gathering ideas and acquainting ourselves with some of the problems of Dry Zone farming. So, working from the main project at Udawelayagama, we went to see farms, projects and people, mounted on our Honda 90 motorbikes. This was a bone-rattling experience on rough roads, but we learned an immense amount. After getting our plans and estimates into presentable form for another meeting, in January 1982, Redd Barna gave us the go-ahead and funds to start up the project.

Our plan was to introduce small livestock like chickens,

rabbits and fish, which could be supported entirely from the holding without having to buy expensive protein or made-up feed. We would keep two bullocks to make muck for the biogas plant which would, in turn, produce gas fuel for ourselves and good manure for the farm. The cost of the ponds, which would have to be lined because of the porous soil, would be met by the second crop of fish in June 1983, and by using the water for irrigation in July and August. In addition, we planned to try out silos of different designs to reduce grain storage losses, and to build a clay cooking stove, a smoker for fish and perhaps rabbit meat, a solar drier for grain, pulses and grapes, and possibly a wind pump to lift water from the ponds. We envisaged our crops including maize and ground-nuts, khurrakan, other millets, and pulses (including soya) to feed the rabbits and chickens. For the cattle we planned to grow some experimental Dry Zone grasses, legumes and fodder trees. Ideas for cash crops developed, and we are now trying papaws for papain production (a medical drug made from dried papaya), grapes and passion fruit, and some capsicums and gherkins, for which there is a ready market.

There is nothing new in any of these things individually, but we thought it would be useful to get them going as an integrated unit in the context of the project – a two-and-a-half acre plot of Dry Zone jungle, with water limited to about 300 gallons per day, very high transport costs, and, most troublesome of all, free-ranging goats, cattle, and elephants. Our budget, which included all material inputs to the holding, transport, labour costs and our own salaries, was less than £60 per week. Cash from the sale of produce goes to Redd Barna's office for redistribution.

The newly resettled village of Udawelayagama is spread out along three lanes half a mile from the old village. There are fifty holdings, each of two and a half acres, with a house built by the occupants. Redd Barna supplied the village with materials, agricultural inputs, and subsistence wages until the first harvest in January 1982. Our project was to run separate from, but in co-operation with, the village as a whole.

From an agricultural point of view, the aim of the project in the long term is to show that a living *can* be made from permanent cultivation of two and a half acres, and that chena cultivation is wasteful of manpower and land resources. Farmers are rightly slow to change tried and trusted techniques. Now, a year after starting the project and (like the rest of the village) having had so much destroyed by everything from elephants to viruses, we understand their lack of enthusiasm for long-term practices of good husbandry. Add to this the effects of the Yala wind blowing night and day for three and a half dry months, and heavy monsoon rains from October to December (both of which carry away any topsoil left uncovered by vegetation), and one can appreciate the scale of problems the villagers faced.

Our holding lies on the edge of the village, across an elephant road. Nothing daunted, we moved into a pre-fabricated plywood house which Redd Barna had built for us, and set about clearing and fencing. At least this would keep out water buffalo, cattle and goats. The traditional fence consists of a line of vertical poles and sticks with one horizontal bar; to keep out young goats, poles have to be placed very close together, and finally we made it 'stock-proof' – apart from elephants, that was!

Starting in January meant that we had missed the main growing season, but there was still plenty to do. We dug two fish ponds of 12,000 gallons each and stocked them with tilarpia and two kinds of Chinese carp, to make a poly-cultural system. We also built a house over each pond for chickens and rabbits, whose droppings fertilized the ponds and supplied the fish with food. Bananas, pawpaws and grass cuttings were planted, and half an acre of cowpeas tilled. The biogas tank was built ready for use when we had grass enough to feed the bullocks to fill it. We built Mark I and II cooking stoves from ant-hill clay and sand, with moveable chimneys, a very useful innovation with wet wood or a high wind. Our eldest son stayed with us for a month, and Turf and he built the first grain silo out of ferro-cement, though this later proved too expensive.

189

We grew aquatic ferns on the ponds and dried them to supplement the protein in the chicken and rabbit diet; later we made a fish trap and now feed the rapidly breeding small tilarpia back to the chicken for protein. Throughout the dry period we gradually cleared the ground, leaving undergrowth lying on the surface, and refusing many suggestions to burn it off (as was the usual practice).

It took the village people a short while, and the Redd Barna staff a little longer, to get used to the idea that we were quite happy to work in the field, mix concrete, build pens and cookers and do many of the small jobs which occur daily on the farm. We actually employ two or three women regularly, and two men when there is building work to be done, and this labour force represents the 'family labour' which would be available for farm work in any of the village households. Even then we miss out a bit on children who, on the villagers' farms, fetch the firewood and keep watch during the day against marauding parakeets and small birds. In addition to their day-time work, the men of the household keep night watch when there are crops in the ground, and the village often echoes to their shouts and to bangers which are of some help in deterring elephants.

Quite often, we also have to do these night watches. Turf takes over from me at midnight, having had a short sleep, and, armed with bangers and a concentrated beam torch, he watches from the barn by the light of a fire. Elephants are difficult to see in the dark and they move quite silently, only the odd crack of timber betraying their presence. One night, before we knew the ropes, we had an elephant not four yards from our house. He was so close that, looking out of the door, we did not realize at first that the darkness was, in fact, elephant! We watched him, fascinated, for an hour and a half, demolishing our banana trees and water melons. He was too close to argue with.

During those dry months, we had time to take records of wells and water pumps in three neighbouring villages, in order to try to raise funds for a tube-well and hand-pump for each one. Redd Barna were keen to spread their assistance more widely in the district and were pleased that we raised funds from Water Aid to enable their drilling rig (another Redd Barna project) to install the wells and pumps. The rig had first been used to drill four tube-wells at Udawelayagama in November 1981, and Turf divined the exact site for the wells. We also sent some proposals to the field office, hoping to corner some funds from the British High Commission to finance a carpenter's workshop and tools for the village. Unfortunately we were unlucky.

The major social and community events of village life allow us the chance to join in with our neighbours. Over Sinhalese New Year (in April), the village resounds with the noise of bangers, and we were overwhelmed with little cakes that had been brought as presents. The Prime Minister came in June to open the Community Hall and hand out the land titles to individual farmers; we lent our chairs and tape-cutting scissors for the occasion, and during a community development week we were asked to open the proceedings and run some games. We have since opened the community shop too, the first step towards the collective marketing which is so essential to a stable farming area.

Many visitors, official and unofficial, come to be shown round the farm, and we explain to them our individual projects and our overall aims. People from the village are around the farm constantly, as we think these informal visits are more effective than formal seminars and talks, so in the remaining nine months of our service we intend to concentrate on passing on the details and aims of the project to Redd Barna staff, villagers, and anyone else who is interested, through a series of practical demonstrations.

Turf's 'First Aid Time' (5 p.m.) arose spontaneously from the peoples' interest in us and our wish to get to know them personally. It consists mainly in attending to cuts, sores and accidents, although quite often it is simply an occasion for chatter and games with the children. We have had some more dramatic incidents, including dressing knife wounds at 11 p.m.

191

on election night, a battered wife, a kwashiokor case, and a call to deliver a baby. Turf was prepared for the emergency, but luckily our Field Officer was staying that night and took the patient to Habarana in the VSO van. On another occasion, a rabid dog bit our dog and several others, and, ten days later, a little girl. We were very surprised how much we had to push to get the authorities to take action about the dogs while Turf took the girl to hospital for a course of injections. For three weeks in October 1982 we had a flow of people running temperatures of 104°F to 105°F, and we were continually dishing out aspirins and bathing heads and bodies; we finally succumbed ourselves. Since then Turf has been giving basic first-aid lessons to the community health workers about home treatment of fevers, wounds and general hygiene, with the aid of David Werner's *'Where There is no Doctor'* and the VSO *Health Handbook*, by Gervase Hamilton.

When the rains came, on 17 September 1982, we started our first season of cultivation. We had the luck to strike the first good monsoon for eight years, which meant that the village tank overflowed and rice would be grown again in the village paddy field of about ten acres. It also meant heavy rainstorms, washouts and very bad roads. We fetch almost all our household and project supplies on motorbikes, either from Habarana (five miles) or Dambulla (fifteen miles away). This includes bags of cement, lengths of timber, rolls of wire netting, chickens, rabbits and many other things. Washed-out roads are difficult with heavy loads but the motor-bikes never let us down.

It was during November, when the crops were coming on well, that the elephants really began to take their toll – their due, perhaps, for our being on their road. We had twenty-six break-ins between 10 November and 20 December, and our maize, khurrakan, and thanna hal were almost completely destroyed. The fence, which had been strengthened with glyricidia cuttings for fodder, needed repairing to 'goat-proof' standard almost every morning, and we began to feel less well-disposed towards elephants! The break-ins continued at a

192

slightly lower intensity until February, when the main herd of about thirty moved away. We left our 'family' in charge of the farm while we spent Christmas near Trincomalee, much appreciating the break.

After a New Year's party in the village at a neighbour's house, we started making silage, much to the amusement of the villagers, who were as incredulous about the procedure as they are about the biogas, which is now brewing in the tank and will shortly be making gas for our cooking and lighting.

And so, as we write, we have reached the fifteen month 'mile-post', and it is time to take stock. Of course there have been difficulties and delays, but we have had good results from the fish ponds; the hens are laying well; and the rabbits (now thirty-seven of them) are to be incorporated into a rabbit-rearing scheme for the village and other Redd Barna projects, using my cage designs. Turf's second silo, now storing our grain, is also going to be used elsewhere, and our smoked fish is good and keeping well. My cooking stove is in constant use, and we have many requests for plans for it and for the smoker, the silo, and the cattle yokes in the bull shed. We still have the solar drier and the wind pump to build, and will be having a try at trickle irrigation under the dry windy conditions of the Yala season. Finally, we hope to try out the effectiveness of carbide guns and donkeys as elephant-deterrents!

Integrated? Well perhaps not quite yet, but we expect to be so when the biogas is functioning and the drier built. Two years is a very short time for an agricultural project, and whether we shall see the papain or the grapes harvested before we go is uncertain.

The problems for village farmers in the dry zone are many and various and we are learning all the time, but we think that some of the new possibilities and aspects of farming that we are demonstrating will be of value both to Udawelayagama and elsewhere. We have been accustomed, through twenty-five years of farm life, to improvising and adjusting to unexpected circumstances, and being continually on call is nothing new to us; this has given us an affinity with the people we are working with, and, in spite of our very basic Sinhala, we have found no difficulty in communicating – except with the elephants!

24

GILLIAN RADCLIFFE. Born 1956, Douglas, Isle-of-Man. Before VSO worked as a scientific officer for the Nature Conservatory Council, and as an Assistant Ranger, National Trust for Scotland. She is currently working as a Park Interpretation Officer at the Bako National Park, Sarawak, Malaysia.

BAKO NATIONAL Park occupies a peninsula on the coast of Sarawak, about half a day's journey by boat from Kuching, the capital. It's an exceptionally beautiful area scenically, with rugged sandstone cliffs all round the coastal boundary, interspersed with small bays. Superb views of Santubong mountain, on the opposite side of the bay from Telok Assam (the park HQ) are a daily feature – weather permitting! The area was originally designated a National Park for its scenery, botanical variety (there are many different vegetation types characteristic of Sarawak within the relatively small area, about 6,750 acres, of the park), and of course its wildlife, which includes the bizarre-looking Proboscis monkey, unique to Borneo. It's a very exciting place to be from the scientific point of view.

Living facilities are good. I live in a comfortable wooden house which was new when I arrived (in fact completed a month or so after I moved in), and have running water (although it was in very short supply towards the end of the dry season last year), and electricity in the evenings (when the generator works). This machine is the one thing I really dislike about being in Bako: I far prefer it when it has broken down, and we use pressure lamps and candles. Then there's a chance

194

to hear the night noises of the forest.

Our park community is shared between the human and the animal raiders. The long-tailed macaques are a real menace. Visitors think they are so endearing (and a few are) and feed them, so they have become very bold and cheeky. They'll enter our kitchens – some even when we're inside – and steal anything vaguely edible. You can't leave your house open for a moment. You soon get to know the individual personalities – some are really obnoxious! I'm engaged in continual psychological warfare with one particular young male and I'm not at all sure that he's not getting the upper hand!

Our human community of about twenty or so (the numbers vary) lives at Telok Assam. Four Forest Guards, one of whom is in overall charge, see to the general running of the park. Then there are boat drivers, carpenters and labourers, some with wives and children. I find the staff of the park a very friendly crowd, and we get on well, though I'll never be quite one of them. I'm sure that they find me, and the work I do, a little on the eccentric side!

During the dry season we have a fairly constant stream of visitors, but in the rainy season (as now) we're cut off and the park is very peaceful. The sea has been very rough for the past month and getting in and out is at times a dodgy business, so running short of food supplies can be a bit of a problem. Even so, I still get to Kuching every few weeks to use the facilities there – the libraries, the museum and so on, so I'm hardly deprived socially.

A high proportion of my time is spent in the forest. Perhaps this means I run a high risk of accident, but I'm sure I'm far safer walking here than crossing the road in town! There are poisonous snakes in the park (cobras, apparently) though I've yet to see one, and pit vipers are fairly common, but they're pretty sluggish and mild-tempered, so no real threat. I think the main danger lies in slipping down somewhere and breaking a leg, but there's no greater risk of accident than there would be hill-walking in England. Anyway, if I was expected back by nightfall and didn't show up, someone would come looking.

The dangers of the tropical forest are so often greatly sensationalized. Although sometimes a little uncomfortable, sweaty and full of mosquitoes and rottans (which are very sharp), the forest is usually benevolent, a marvellous place in which to live and work. The sea tends to hold more dangers than the forest. We have a lot of jelly-fish in the dry season, and quite a few people get severely stung, so it's a little off-putting. Occasionally people step on stingrays, or on catfish with poisonous spines. But I've not yet heard of anyone being bitten by a sea-snake!

My work is to interest visitors who come to the park and educate them about its wildlife, and the need for conservation. But before you can inform people about the park, it's necessary to have a reasonably comprehensive and scientifically accurate picture of what is there. So, basic groundwork has involved a lot of inventory work, recording birds, mammals and so on. This, of course, is a continuous process, and takes up a lot of time. While out doing this work, gradually forming a mental picture of the park, its most interesting features, habitats and so on, for future interpretation, I've also been building up a photographic record. So far I have about six hundred slides and intend to take many more. I've just been sorting some out so that I can assemble an introductory slideshow about the park, which I hope the World Wildlife Fund is going to produce, and to select others for enlargement into displays and posters for the Park Information Centre. The Centre is to be extended this year, and I'm busy reorganizing that – designing and making new displays, and giving it a complete overhaul. I'm also writing leaflets on various aspects of the park for distribution to visitors. The Information Centre tries to provide visitors with a lively introduction to the park and will, I hope, stress what they can (rather than what they cannot) do while they are there. They'll be fully encouraged to use the excellent system of trails to explore the park. Paths were originally set up over twenty years ago, and have been extended and improved with time. The trails are very well maintained by the staff, but are under-utilized. The expanded Centre will also cover the geology and geomorphology of the area (which lends itself very well to displays, since Bako is so visually attractive). Different habitat types – mangroves, dipterocarpus forest, the seashore and so on, will be covered next, in the planned exhibition, their development being related back to the geology and geomorphology of the area. The final section will be more general, looking at other parks in Sarawak, why we need them, and so forth. I hope to get the messages across as visually as possible.

In the future I hope to arrange some on-site interpretation in certain selected areas. I would also like to set up a fairly short, circular nature trail passing through the different kinds of mangrove forest. But that would require construction of a very long, raised walkway, and would therefore be very expensive, so I don't know if we can go ahead with this idea or not. Although hostels and camping sites are provided in the park, we don't want to over-develop the area; it is, after all, a National Park, not a holiday camp. Most visitors are local people, which is as it should be: they often come in great numbers on public holidays, the majority just to be by the seaside, play music, and picnic. Sadly, they don't yet come because the place is a park; that is where my work comes in.

Visitors without their own transport (almost all) must stay at least one night at Telok Assam, so in a sense we have a captive audience. For educational work we can capitalize on this, since most people enjoy having something laid on for them in the evening, particularly a slide show. It's a good opportunity to try and stimulate their interest and also to chat to them informally.

Since I have no local counterpart at the park itself, I have to limit myself to doing fairly straightforward things which can be easily maintained and kept going after my departure. So there's no point in my being over-ambitious and setting up (for example) programmes for school groups, as there simply won't be anyone there to carry on for many years to come. Still, the Forest Guards are very capable, and once I've produced slide shows with a taped commentary, they're quite able to run them and answer questions. The nearest person to a direct counter-

197

part is based in Kuching, who joined the Section six months ago as a 'Park Interpreter', a new post. He will be responsible for education and extension work in all the parks – a huge job which really needs more than one person. It's unfortunate that we're based in separate places, as it greatly limits our chances to work together. Still, I'm hoping that later he'll be coming to Bako more often, and perhaps before I leave we can spend some months together working out interpretive plans for the different parks. As long as the groundwork at Bako has been well carried out, it should make his job simpler. He should be able to visit, say, twice a year, to update or alter displays, and determine future developments.

In terms of the project's contribution to development, the position is less clear. Basically I feel that any work which tries to increase the level of environmental awareness of the general public (and politicians, decisions-makers and others) is for the good. On the whole there is very little understanding here of important issues such as the effects of extensive forest clearance due to agriculture and logging (and its associated environmental degradation) or of pollution, let alone of the need for wildlife conservation. The environment is all too often a casualty of development. I feel there's little value in putting aid and money into developments which are potentially harmful in the long term, unless an awareness of the damage that can be done, and of ways of preventing and counteracting it, is fostered at the same time. So rapidly developing countries do need to educate people, and to encourage concern, in order to limit potential damage to the environment.

Fortunately, despite a lot of awareness at public level, there are a number of enlightened individuals in government service (particularly in the Forest Department), who see the need for careful management of resources for long-term benefit – including, of course, conservation. The very fact that a project like mine exists is an encouraging sign, and in fact another VSO, Hugh Watson, is carrying out wildlife survey work in Niah and Lambir Hills Parks. A Canadian volunteer has been in Niah for three years in a similar job to mine. There are already five parks in Sarawak, with more on the way. The long-term survival of the parks cannot be ensured, however, unless they gain public support. If they do not, they will lose out amid increasing pressures on the land which are growing on every site. Educating the public about environmental conservation in the broadest sense is therefore of paramount importance. There is undoubtedly a tremendous amount to be done, but Sarawak does have the potential to be an exemplary country in terms of good environmental management. I just hope that this potential can be realized.

25

ANNA SZUMINSKA. Born 1955, Southport, Lancashire. Received her B.Ed. and Diploma in special education from Preston Polytechnic, before becoming a teacher of the educationally sub-normal at Forest Oak School in Birmingham. In 1981 she applied to VSO and was posted to the School for the Mentally Handicapped in Kuching, Sarawak, Malaysia. Anna is working in Kuching while a local teacher is trained in the UK.

THE SCHOOL for the mentally retarded in Kuching, Sarawak was started ten years ago with just a few pupils and one teacher. It has grown slowly to its present size of seventy children. As a result of funds from the Year of the Disabled, all day pupils now arrive by mini bus or car. We are also in our own building, which has been open for just over a year.

The school was started and has been developed over the years by the Social Welfare Council, consisting of representatives from The Salvation Army, the Cheshire Homes, the Red Crescent and many others, even including the Sarawak Society for the Prevention of Cruelty to Animals. The Council is constantly appealing for donations and has been very successful in its fund raising. At the moment the Council is channelling all its funds into the construction of another new building. This will have more classrooms, a hall, hopefully a physiotherapy room, and offices for the Council's use. The school is funded from voluntary donations, with the Ministry of Education financing my salary and 90 per cent of the other two teachers' wages.

So what am I doing here? What I know can be done and what I am doing are two very different things. Ideally, there should only be about eight to ten children in a class, with one full-time helper. With such a small number I would then be able to draw up individual programmes of learning for each child, based on an assessment and analysis of all areas of development. This would include their levels of receptive and expressive language development, cognitive development, and so on. However, with twenty-four mostly very active younger and lower ability children in my class this year, such a plan of work is impossible. Instead, I am trying to implement group work, and we do a lot of play. By this I mean we utilize the whole of the classroom and as much equipment and salvaged cartons, plastic bottles or yoghourt pots as possible, rather than expecting children to sit at their individual desks with a piece of paper or a toy. Many of the children are at the same stage as any other young child who needs movement alongside other stimulation. Although we do spend time sitting at our desks, this is not the main emphasis.

Of course, there are inevitably problems with managing group activities. Because of their slower development, mentally handicapped children can often be very egocentric. They see the environment as revolving around themselves. If they want somebody else's bricks they will take them without any regard for other children. Despite these problems, play is a great thing for social development. The children learn about having to share equipment, to take turns and take account of each other. When I talk about play, I don't mean a free-for-all, letting them get on with it themselves. You have to be in there with them and use play as a medium to direct their activities. In

200

this way play can be used to help them learn how to recognize, understand and order their experiences. Of course, with twenty-four in the class you can only be with a few at a time. But the others do manage to utilize the classroom!

Our day here begins with a visit to the toilet. A few of the children are not toilet trained, and others don't always remember to go! Some don't know how to use the toilet properly. We then return to the classroom and sit on the floor together and sing 'Good Morning to You' and shake hands with each other, trying to encourage social interaction, especially with the more withdrawn children. After this we usually play with 'play-dough', a substance which constantly reappears throughout the day in all sorts of places! It has a soft texture, and I try to get the children to explore its properties and potential, rolling it into sausages, making balls, sticking fingers in it, lifting it into the air and letting it dribble down. Not only is it good for the co-ordination of hand and eye, for language development, and for encouraging imitation, it's also fun.

A couple of the children make representational shapes, but for most of them it's far too early to expect this. It takes a high level of development in a child to be able to know objects and then produce them in representational form – a recognizable form, that is! Some children are only just moving it about between their fingers. When the children decide they've had enough they clean up and move to another activity, such as building bricks. I usually have one of the amahs (helpers) with me, one who enjoys the play-dough activity. While she sits with them I work with a few others, particularly the non-verbal ones. I try to encourage things like blowing, the imitation of gestures such as clapping and so on, generally trying to develop language skills and cognition.

As far as possible we try to stick to a set routine during the day. It's very important for the children to have the security of a basic daily pattern. They need to know what's going to happen and what they have to do. They will get too confused if there is total change every day. Having a routine gives stability and security and also means they can be successful within an

201

established structure. New things can be introduced slowly without causing too much confusion.

Our main objective is to develop the children's skills. Most of them have no language. Some just make noises, which is a start, as at least they see the need to make them. I've already mentioned some of the pre-language activities, but I also want to establish in the children's minds a need for communication. For example, at break-time when they want coffee, holding out their cup is communication if it's trying to attract my attention. I hope that some of them will later give a one-word response or a gesture. Some may never develop speech, so I hope we may be able to establish a small sign vocabulary, and some may just not be ready yet. Of course this means a lot of individual work, which with twenty-four children is going to be minimal.

Last year's class were the total opposite of this year's. They were older and more capable, and there were only eight in the class. However, they were all using language as any other child their age might do, which meant that I needed their language in order to teach them. I wasn't very fluent in Chinese or Malay and although the children learnt a lot of English it wasn't sufficient for learning advanced concepts. But one notable case of social (and possibly emotional) development stands out. The boy in question has a history of a broken home, of life in a children's home, and of then being returned to his father and new stepmother. As with most children who have no stable relationship, or no stable home life in their early years, he was, and is, quite disturbed, though still of 'normal' intelligence. I think he was brought to our school originally because of his behaviour and because he had never learned to read. He could be very disruptive in class, throwing things around, tormenting other children and so on. He refused to do what he was asked. But at other times he would show great pleasure in conversing with me. After a year of many battles and learning that as with other things, I meant 'pick your rubbish up off the floor' when I said it, we established quite a good two-way relationship. Although even now he still finds it necessary to act aggressively to other children, I think a tremendous change has taken place in his attitude to myself and to Claire, the volunteer who was here last year. He will actually approach and open up a conversation in his quite well-developed English (obviously picked up during last year); he asks about pictures in newspapers, and every morning he still asks me to tell him a story from the books in my room.

We have made progress like this because children need people to show an interest in them; people who listen and talk with gentle understanding, and with a disciplined rather than authoritarian approach. This is what they find at our school.

Of course, the attitude of individuals and the community outside school is equally important. The boy in my example may well, for example, end up in prison; outside school he is apparently quite an active vandal. I think his behaviour and needs are beyond the general understanding of his community.

On the other hand, Malaysian parents are generally very protective towards their children. Some are so protective that they hinder their child's development, not realizing the great potential their children have for development, and in some cases merely increasing their children's handicaps. This is of course mainly because the parents love their children and are not aware of the possibilities of what can be done. One way of getting round this problem is through the Parent-Teacher Association, which we are at present setting up. I hope to be able to show a few films and maybe run a workshop or two. I'd like to be able to show the parents how to help their children develop their potential. The trouble is that many people are rather suspicious of any deviation from the traditional style of classroom management – the style which mostly consists of children sitting still at their desks.

In addition, parents in this part of the world don't seem to share in the problems of their children, often merely carrying on regardless. I don't know if the PTA will encourage the airing and discussion of such things; I hope so. It is true that, as in England, there is now a growing trend for parents to be involved together with teachers in the classroom. It's early days yet in the development of our school, but we hope something similar will catch on in the near future, because an effective PTA could also help to promote a better understanding of retarded children in society at large. I believe that parents' desire for a better life for their children will in turn lead to self-education. It must be our hope that long-established misconceptions of mental handicap as a disease will gradually disappear, as people come to realise that it is a permanent condition in which there is room for tremendous improvement, rather than an illness to be treated by medical care.

26

PAUL UNWIN. Born 1955, Stockport, Cheshire. Studied at Huddersfield Polytechnic, where he was Deputy President of the Students' Union. He then worked as a Welfare Assistant, and as an Engineering Technician for Lawrence Scott Limited. He joined VSO in 1982, and is currently serving as a Technical Officer with the Village Industry Research and Training Unit, Arawa, North Solomons Province, Papua New Guinea.

THE UNFAMILIAR southern skies seemed to take on a milky radiance from more stars than I had ever thought to see. An almost full moon beamed cheerfully, and a pleasantly cool breeze from somewhere in the north-east carried the chatterings of hosts of tiny insects. The tropical night slowly enveloped us as we sat on the veranda enjoying an after-dinner drink and a smoke in good company. Sounds a little like paradise, albeit in a rather colonial mould? It was.

No matter that the veranda, indeed the entire house, was built of leaves and timbers gathered within stone-throwing distance. No matter that the dinner had been the ubiquitous tinned fish and rice, the coffee instant, and the smoke barely-cured leaf from the garden. No matter too that the company was barely able to converse: Thomas and his brother spoke English little better than my own faltering Tok Pisin, and Thomas's wife was too shy to do other than hover in the background. The day's work was done, ideas had already been exchanged, and polite attempts to chat had gradually lapsed into a companionable silence. For me, these things only added magic to the evening.

So why was I there? The Village Industry Research and Training Unit (or VIRTU) had been asked by the North Solomons' Provincial Government Department of Primary Industry to investigate a problem faced by local farmers and smallholders. It seemed that the fragile long-leafed Chinese cabbage was all too often damaged by being bounced around in the back of a pick-up on the bush 'roads' going to market. The farmers' revenue was suffering badly. Some kind of container into which cabbages could be tightly packed seemed to be called for, but the polypropylene boxes available as imports from Australia were rather expensive. However, a number of people in the Siwai and Buin districts of south-west Bougainville were making furniture from the local cane known as kunda – why should they not also make a rattan basket for the farmers?

Thomas Kunai provided the answer. Thomas is about twenty-seven years old, softly-spoken and slight in stature. He had learned his craft at the Vocational School in Buin, but had little inclination to start his own cane workshop. The copper mines offered more lucrative employment. But the money had palled after six years of eighty-hour weeks in the mess kitchen and living in a tiny and inescapably noisy cubicle, so Thomas had gone back to his village. He found his brother and a number of friends in trouble with the law, largely as a result of their frustrated aspirations. Apart from the mine, there aren't many 'modern' employment opportunities in the North Solomons. So Thomas, with a little business help from an uncle who runs the nearby trade store, started to make cane furniture, passing on his skills to his brother and four friends who work with him. His enterprise did more than keep them out of trouble and provide a little income: it has developed to the point where a new workshop, with ten rather than five staff, is about to open. I wanted Thomas to make a kunda basket for the farmers.

The drive between the grand metropolis of Arawa, where VIRTU is based, and Thomas's village in Siwai, is not restful. Water from three forded rivers had lapped over the little 'ute' (utility vehicle), ponderous climbs and daunting descents had tried the engine, transmission and brakes, and the suspension had been tested quite unreasonably. But we pressed relentlessly on (just as others did, as the number of other vehicles which blithely passed us by seemed to suggest). After our arrival we worked our way through some ideas and finished up with a promising and workable prototype. We were pretty pleased with it (and ourselves), and there was an interesting atmosphere to our soirée that evening.

Beneath that calm tranquillity was a sense of potential, of movement, of vitality, of validity, of authenticity, and, I like to think, of shared respect. I think we all felt our prototype basket was far from perfect, but it did seem to point the way to a serviceable, viable product which might generate income and reduce reliance on an import. We felt we were headed in the right direction on that first afternoon, and were enthusiastic about the morrow. Thomas never told me how he felt about the idea of trying to meet a local need rather than pandering to the whims of a vagarious luxury (and largely expatriate) market with his furniture. Maybe he never thought about it at all, and it would be idle of me to read radical ideals into something which for him was just a job; or perhaps not. At any rate, he was pleased by the prospect of diversity. I use words like validity and authenticity to suggest no more than the feeling (on my part at least) that we were engaged in a project of some value – value, that is, by some universal standard. I recall being told as an apprentice that the electric motors I was working on were to power torpedoes: such work may arguably also have its merits, but they would be quite unlike the sense of validity that evening in Siwai, and I know which of the two I prefer.

But this tells you nothing of the country of Papua New Guinea: of eagles soaring high over the bush, of kingfishers tensely waiting on fallen trees in rivers, of snowy cockatoos disturbed by the roadside, of gaudy parrots perched in trees by the village. It tells you nothing of bright butterflies the size of dinner-plates, of flying squirrels hanging dormant in tree-tops, of beetles which would need a truly family-sized matchbox before they might be captured by curious children. Nor will it tell you much about cloud-shrouded mountains and rolling valleys, nothing of beaches like television advertisements for chocolates and cigars, nor of the inevitable palms and cocoa plantations and a host of other foliage struggling for space and sunlight. All this contributed to the excitement felt by one freshly-arrived volunteer.

I had not then had time to learn the dubious lessons of experience; or to take note of cynical conversations in hotel bars and supermarket cafeterias about how difficult it was actually to 'get anything done' in Papua New Guinea. At that time I hardly recognized the seemingly wilful obstacles placed in the path of 'development' by local politicians. I barely realized the enormous problems created by a poor communications infrastructure. No, in those early days I was filled with awe at the splendour of a magnificent country, infatuated by a misguided and probably dangerous romanticism, and wrapped up in my very first project which, though it might please a few locals, would in reality hardly scratch the surface of national development problems. I was still amazed by the existence of roads at all, let alone the comprehensive network which would allow almost any settlement to be reached by a determined driver in a four-wheel-drive utility vehicle. The fact that there were few telephones seemed to matter infinitely less than the notion that the lines were far clearer than in the UK, and outstations had a very impressive radio system. There were no post-boxes, but a letter posted in one of the many post offices would reach its destination faster and more cheaply than in England. The extremely well-developed system of schools and community governments seemed to offer excellent channels for communicating developmental ideas, by means of the first-class local radio service.

Each day seemed to offer new discoveries about my environment, both natural and social, and about myself. Apart from the odd twinge of nostalgia for all I had left behind I felt only gratitude for the opportunity to try to do something I believed to be of worth in such idyllic surroundings.

This, as I say, was in my early days as a volunteer, when I was touched by the gracious hospitality extended to me by such as Thomas, by their appreciation of the efforts which had brought me to them (of which my own may well have been the least). I was overwhelmed by their friendliness, flattered by their interest, and sometimes embarrassed by their unwarranted faith in what the late Lord Butler called 'the art of the possible'.